Birth to Three Matters

BIRTH TO THREE MATTERS: Supporting the Framework of Effective Practice

Lesley Abbott and Ann Langston

Open University Press

Open University Press
McGraw-Hill Education
McGraw-Hill House
Shoppenhangers Road
Maidenhead
Berkshire
England
SL6 2QL

email: enquiries@openup.co.uk
world wide web: www.openup.co.uk

and Two Penn Plaza, New York, NY 10121–2289, USA

First published 2005
Reprinted 2005

A catalogue record of this book is available from the British Library

ISBN 0 335 21540 8 (pb) 0 335 21541 6 (hb)

Library of Congress Cataloging-in-Publication Data
CIP data applied for

Typeset by YHT Ltd, London
Printed in the UK by Bell & Bain Ltd., Glasgow

This book is dedicated to all babies, children, their parents and all those who work with them.

Contents

List of Contributors

Lesley Abbott is Professor of Early Childhood Education at the Institute of Education at Manchester Metropolitan University. She directed the *Birth to Three Matters* project for the DfES. She also directed the earlier research project *Educare for the Under Threes*, which resulted in the training and resource materials *Shaping the Future – Working with the Under Threes*. She has a background in primary and early childhood education and has worked in teacher education and multidisciplinary training for many years developing one of the first Early Childhood Studies degrees. She has served on a number of government committees and contributed to conferences nationally and internationally. She has worked in Australia, Singapore and Ireland and has published widely in the early years field. Publications include *Working with the Under Threes – Training and Professional Development* and *Working with the Under Threes – Responding to Children's Needs, Early Education Transformed* with Helen Moylett and, co-edited with Gillian Pugh, *Training to Work in the Early Years – Developing the Climbing Frame*. She is currently directing the *Birth to Three Training Matters* project funded by the Esmée Fairbairn Foundation and recently received a Lifetime Achievement Award alongside Lesley Staggs.

Ian Barron is Principal Lecturer in Early Childhood Education at the Manchester Metropolitan University. He is a member of the national Early Childhood Studies Degrees Network. He has had a variety of experiences in the early childhood field, including work in primary schools in inner London and Leeds and headship of a nursery school in Lancashire and of an infant school in Calderdale. Ian has also provided in-service and advisory services for a number of LEAs, has contributed to the development of early years curriculum guidelines and was a member of the project team that developed the *Birth to Three Matters* Framework. He has also worked in a further education college, as an OFSTED Registered Inspector (Primary), and in a college of higher education. His research interests and journal publications are in the areas of early literacy, training of early childhood workers and constructions of childhood.

Tina Bruce is Honorary Visiting Professor at the University of Surrey Roehampton. Her contribution over the years includes international work in the USA, New Zealand and Europe, and the influence of her specialist training working with children with special educational needs and disability and their families is promoting inclusion. Tina has brought a Froebelian perspective on government committees, including developing the *Curriculum Guidance for the Foundation Stage*, the *Foundation Profile* and the *Birth to Three Matters* Framework. She is author of numerous best-selling books, including *Childcare and Education, Learning Through Play: Babies, Toddlers and the Foundation Years* and *Developing Learning in Early Childhood*. She is editor of *Early Childhood Practice: The Journal for Multi-Professional Partnerships*. She, with Jean Ensing, CBE, recently received the Lifetime Achievement Award at Early Years, 2002.

Tricia David is Emeritus Professor of Education at Canterbury Christ Church University College, having officially retired in 2002. She was a Professor of Education at Canterbury Christ Church University College for seven years and prior to that worked at Warwick University for ten years, having been a headteacher of both nursery and primary schools earlier in her career. Tricia's research and writing is mainly concerned with the earliest years (birth to age 6). She has written or edited thirteen books and has had around one hundred articles published in journals or as chapters in books. Tricia is known internationally for her work with l'Organisation Mondiale pour l'Education Prescolaire (OMEP) and for the OECD, for whom she recently acted as rapporteur of their study of Early Childhood Education and Care in the Netherlands, reported in *Starting Strong* (OECD 2001). She was greatly assisted by her five grandchildren in her work for the *Birth to Three Matters* project.

Pat Djemli is now a Senior Educare Adviser for Staffordshire Early Years and Childcare Unit. Until recently she was the Care Manager at Tamworth Early Years Centre. Her chapter in this book was written with Helen Moylett while they were both still working at Tamworth. Her management responsibilities at the Centre included working with the under 3s and family support. Pat has worked as a nursery nurse and manager in various settings. Before moving to Tamworth Early Years Centre she was the manager of a social services day nursery and has many years of experience working in day care. She has developed parenting programmes and other family support packages which are used across the county. She contributed to 'Ten Steps to Five' (1997), Staffordshire's developmental record for under 5s. Pat is an NVQ Level 3/4 assessor and has almost finished her own NVQ Level 5 in Operational Management. She has a particular interest in young children's views on provision and as an advanced skills practitioner was leading the Centre's work on the Esmée Fairbairn-funded *Birth to Three Training Matters* project.

Bernadette Duffy is Head of the Thomas Coram Early Childhood Centre in Camden, which has been designated as a Sure Start Children's Centre by the DfES. The Centre offers fully integrated care and education for young children in partnership with their parents and the local community. Bernadette was a valued member of the Working Group for the *Birth to Three Matters* project. She was also part of the Qualification and Curriculum Authority (QCA) Foundation Stage working party which devised the *Guidance for the Foundation Stage* and had a particular input into the section on creative development. She is currently involved in an extension to the QCA's *Creativity: Find it: Promote it*. Bernadette is Vice-Chair of the British Association for Early Childhood Education, a fellow of the Royal Society of Arts, a member of the DfES Early Education Advisory Group and the Primary Education Study Group. Bernadette has contributed to a number of publications and is author of *Supporting Creativity and Imagination in the Early Years*, published by Open University Press.

Peter Elfer is Senior Lecturer in Early Childhood Studies at University of Surrey Roehampton. He has undertaken a number of studies of children under 3 in nursery provision and has recently published *Key Persons in Nursery: Building Relationships for Quality Practice* with Elinor Goldschmied and Dorothy Selleck. He was a member of one of the *Birth to Three Matters* working groups. Prior to joining Roehampton, he worked in the Early Childhood Unit at the National Children's Bureau. Peter's current research is looking at how different nurseries manage the emotional complexity of work with babies and children under 3, using the observation method discussed in his chapter of the book.

Kathy Goouch is Team Leader for Early Years Education at Canterbury Christ Church University College. Her interest in young children's literacy has developed over many years' teaching experience, which ranged from kindergarten through the primary stages. Kathy's research focus is in early literacy, particularly in young children's ability to construct meaning through reading and mark-making, and the teaching interactions that support this. Publications include *Making Sense of Early Literacy* (2000) with Tricia David and colleagues involved in the Early Literacy Links Project, and 'Young children and playful language' (with Teresa Grainger) in *Teaching Young Children* (1999) edited by Tricia David. Kathy is currently working with colleagues on research projects relating to creativity and writing, with a consortium of local schools.

Rachel Holmes is a Senior Lecturer and part-time Research Associate at Manchester Metropolitan University. She has a background in teaching in the early years and at Key Stage 1, but has developed an enthusiastic interest in inter-agency working and multiprofessional issues within the early years and has been Course Leader for the BA Early Childhood Studies Degree. Her teaching areas within the University include 'Children's Rights', 'The Individual and the Social in Childhood', 'Teaching Studies' and 'Constructions of Early Childhood'. She has an MA in Arts Education and is currently doing a PhD. Her research is focused around ways of building a therapeutic dimension into teaching and learning for trainee early childhood practitioners.

Julie Jennings is a trained teacher who has specialized in the care and education of children with special educational needs and disabilities. Her postgraduate training has been in working with children who have learning difficulties or visual impairment. She is also a Froebel-trained early childhood teacher. Having taught for many years in special and mainstream schools and early years settings, Julie was head of an LEA visual impairment service before joining RNIB. For RNIB, as Early Years Development Officer, she is taking the lead in promoting services that will improve the range and quality of provision for children under 5 who have a visual impairment, and their families.

Ann Langston is a freelance early years consultant. With a background in teacher education and nursery nurse training, Ann has a wide experience of work and management in the early years. Formerly an Early Years Adviser in a local authority and a Senior Lecturer in Early Years Education, she has managed an Early Years Development and Childcare Partnership as well as having managed under 5s' provision in eight nursery centres and schools in an Early Years Service. Ann was a project team member, involved extensively in the development of the *Birth to Three Matters* Framework (DfES) and also managed the recent *Birth to Three Matters Training of Trainers* Programme (DfES), which included development of the *Birth to Three Childcare Workforce* materials. She has written a number of publications, including curriculum guidelines and early years articles, and has revised a quality assurance scheme for use in under 5s settings. She is currently Project Manager for the Esmée Fairbairn-funded *Birth to Three Training Matters* project based at Manchester Metropolitan University.

Helen Moylett is now a Regional Director for the Foundation Stage, working with local authorities in the West Midlands and the east of England. Until recently she was the Head of Tamworth Early Years Centre in Staffordshire. The Centre provides care and education for children aged 1 to 4 years and support for their families. Her chapter in this book was written with Pat Djemli while they were both still working at Tamworth. Earlier in her career Helen has been a junior, infant, nursery and home–school liaison teacher, a senior advisory teacher and a senior lecturer in early years education at Manchester Metropolitan University. She has co-edited two books on the under 3s with Professor Lesley Abbott as well as *Early Education Transformed* (1999). She contributed a chapter on early years education and care to S. Bartlett and D. Burton (eds) *Education Studies: Essential Issues* (2003). She was Chair of Stockport Early Years Development and Childcare Partnership from

1998 to 2000 and on the national steering group for the *Birth to Three Matters* Framework.

John Powell is Senior Lecturer in Early Childhood Studies at the Institute of Education at Manchester Metropolitan University and has a particular interest in child protection, equal opportunities, children's rights, multiprofessional perspectives and professional development and research. Currently the Second Year Leader of the BA (Hons) in Early Childhood Studies and the Course Leader for two postgraduate degree courses, he is also involved in teaching across a range of levels and subjects relating to childcare and childcare practices. His earlier career as a social worker and as a team manager in education welfare gave him experiences of direct work with families and young children. His current and past involvement in research includes DfES Evaluation of Early Years Excellence Centres and a Teenage Parents Project. He is currently involved with a local EYDCP in research on practices relating to 'touch' in childcare. His PhD was concerned with the construction of identities in schools. Previous research includes work in Belfast and Kirklees. He has produced several articles and chapters for publications and contributed widely to international conferences.

Sacha Powell is Senior Research Fellow in the Centre for Educational Research at Canterbury Christ Church University College. Her research interests, which are strongly influenced by having lived (studied and worked) in the People's Republic of China, include sociocultural constructions of childhood, education in the People's Republic of China, and family education, all with particular reference to the early years of childhood. She is presently engaged in a range of research projects whose foci include modern foreign language learning in primary schools, theoretical underpinnings of learning behaviour, young children's play, and Children's Fund activities in England. Previously, Sacha has worked at the University of Sussex and the British Academy, and in early childhood settings and schools in England, China, Taiwan and Spain.

Gillian Pugh has been Chief Executive of Coram Family since 1997, having previously worked for many years at the National Children's Bureau. Over the past 20 years she has advised governments in the UK and overseas on the development of policy for children, on coordination of services, on prevention and early intervention, on curriculum, and on parent education and support. Gillian was a founder member and is Chair of the Parenting Education and Support Forum and a trustee of the National Family and Parenting Institute. She is an advisor to the Children, Young People and Families directorate within the DfES. She has published many books, including *Contemporary Issues in the Early Years* (three editions), *Confident Parents, Confident*

Children and *Preventative Work with Families*. She co-edited with Lesley Abbott *Training to Work in the Early Years – Developing the Climbing Frame*.

Iram Siraj-Blatchford is Professor of Early Childhood Education at the Institute of Education, University of London. Iram has taught in over 30 countries. She was on the StartRight enquiry and has provided evidence on early education to the National Commission on Education, to local and national governments and the House of Commons Select Committee. She is the co-author of over thirty books, monographs and major published research reports and over a hundred chapters, articles and reports. She is co-director of the major DfES ten-year study on Effective Pre-school and Primary Education (EPPE 3–11) project (1997–2008) and of the Effective Pedagogy in the Early Years project. She is particularly interested in undertaking research that aims to combat disadvantage and to give children and families from disadvantaged backgrounds a head start.

Foreword

I am delighted to write the foreword to *Birth to Three Matters*. The last five years have seen an enormous expansion of childcare for very young children, and, as important, a keen interest by Government in the critical nature of the first five years of childhood. Key developments have been the establishment of the Sure Start Programme, the National Childcare Strategy, and the guarantee of free early education for all 3- and 4-year-olds. Alongside this enormous expansion of service has been a keen concern to ensure the quality of services delivered. In September 2000, the Department for Education and Skills (DfES) introduced the Foundation Stage, a curriculum for 3- , 4- and 5-year-olds that now forms a crucial first part of the National Curriculum. More recently the DfES published the *Birth to Three Matters* Framework, guidance for all those who have responsibility for the care and education of babies and children from birth to 3. Against this wealth of national policy and attention on young children, last autumn the Government published *Every Child Matters*, which sets the basis for the transformation of services for all children, from birth to 19 years of age.

Many in the early years world were gratified at how much *Every Child* *Matters* emphasized the issues that consistently have been part of the early years approach: working with the whole child; bringing together concern for education, social and health outcomes; working with parents as well as children. All these are well reflected in both the Foundation Stage and the *Birth to Three Matters* Framework. Both measures have been widely welcomed in the field, and are making a significant contribution to the quality of children's early experience across the country.

This new book, *Birth to Three Matters*, explores further the structure and content of the *Birth to Three Matters* Framework, giving researchers and practitioners new ways to think about the care and development needs of our youngest children. Many of its contributors were involved in developing both the Foundation Stage and the *Birth to Three Matters* Framework, and all have a long history of working in the early years field.

The quality of children's experiences, and the engagement of their parents, particularly in these early years, is critical to better outcomes that will impact on the child right into adolescence and adulthood. While we have done much to expand quantity, we also must keep working on quality. This book is a key tool for both practitioners delivering services and managers designing and commissioning them.

Naomi Eisenstadt
Director
Sure Start Unit
Department for Education and Skills

Acknowledgements

We are grateful to colleagues at the Sure Start Unit at the DfES, members of the Steering and Working Groups, and the many early years practitioners who have worked so tirelessly with us during the development of the *Birth to Three Matters* Framework, and have so warmly welcomed us into their settings.

We thank the contributors to this book, who have supported us in so many ways and continue to do so.

To the policy makers, parents and partnerships who have shared their views with us, we owe a debt of gratitude.

Most importantly, we say 'thank you' to all the babies and young children who made our work so enjoyable.

Above all, we acknowledge our indebtedness to Caroline Bradbury, Project Administrator, without whose skill, enthusiasm and unfailing good humour, this book, and indeed many of the *Birth to Three Matters* materials, would not have been produced.

Lesley Abbott and Ann Langston

1 Framework Matters

Ann Langston and Lesley Abbott

Introduction

Understanding the needs of very young children and how best to meet them has long been a concern of those who recognize the importance of children's earliest experiences in shaping their future. Gillian Pugh identifies this as one of the main policy challenges. The acceptance by the community of early years practitioners and policy makers of the *Birth to Three Matters* Framework (DfES 2002) and materials, and the overwhelming evidence of its effects on practice, are both heart warming and encouraging to those who, in September 2001, accepted the invitation to develop a framework of 'best practice' (DfEE 2001: para 2.19) to support practitioners working with children from birth to 3 years.

The *Birth to Three Matters* Framework (DfES 2002) is the subject of this chapter. It highlights some of the challenges we faced as Project Director and Manager in accepting the invitation and traces the development of the materials, including the political context in which it took place.

Birth to Three Matters

This chapter explores a number of issues surrounding the publication of *Birth to Three Matters* (DfES 2002). Whilst the Framework pack does not itself constitute a curriculum, it nevertheless emphasizes new thinking about the importance of children aged from birth to 3 and indicates a major shift in the ways in which this age group should be viewed, since traditionally young children's welfare has been a private, rather than a public, concern. It considers changing conceptions of childhood and child development in relation to children up to the age of 3 years and explores the process of research underpinning the Framework. Some of the challenges faced and the issues raised in characterizing the child in 'broad areas of development' are discussed. Finally, the chapter presents an exploration of the Framework itself.

Early childhood care and education in the UK has seen remarkable changes in policy, provision and practice during the last decade, as detailed fully in Chapter 3; changes that have had a profound effect on the lives of young children and their families. This wide-ranging policy agenda has led to an impressive number of initiatives and developments which have had a considerable impact on young children and families, and particularly on those who work with and for them. One of the most encouraging developments has been the government's commitment to 'develop a framework of best practice for supporting children between the ages birth to 3' (DfEE 2001: para 2.19).

Having established that a framework of **effective** rather than **best** practice was more appropriate, the task of its development fell to Professor Lesley Abbott and her team based at the Manchester Metropolitan University (MMU), who, whilst realizing the challenges and responsibilities this would entail, were not, at that stage, aware of their extent.

In liaison with the Department for Education and Skills (DfES)/Sure Start Unit, Steering and Working Groups were established, whose members were representative of a whole range of sectors, departments, organizations and communities, including researchers, practitioners, writers and interest groups committed to the provision of high-quality care and education for children from birth to 3.

The brief was to produce a framework of effective practice to support all those working with young children from birth to 3; to produce materials in hard copy, capable of electronic delivery, together with a review of the literature and research, which would underpin and inform the development of the Framework. The timescale for the project was one year, from 1 September 2001 to 31 August 2002.

Many challenges faced the project team, not least of which were the demands of the short timescale and the size of the task. No wonder then that the support of a team of highly respected early childhood experts, academics, specialists and experienced practitioners was required on a regular basis. In determining what would go into a framework of effective practice it became clear that the starting point should be the child, and many debates centred around the issues of childhood, children between birth and 3, and child development.

Childhood

Childhood is a dynamic concept, depending to a great extent upon the context in which it is defined, and the philosophical premise upon which it is based. Some theorists argue that childhood is 'neither a natural nor universal feature of human groups but – a specific structural and cultural component of many societies' (James and Prout 1997: 8). Whilst others suggest that it is more helpful to talk about 'children who live within a defined area – whether in terms of time, space, economics or other relevant criteria ... [and who]

have a number of characteristics in common' (Qvortrup et al. 1994: 5). Childhood, then, is a problematic concept, but, for the purposes of this chapter, and indeed of this book, will be considered in relation to children in England, at the beginning of the second millennium, in daycare settings, and who are aged from birth to 3 years, which we will refer to as the period of early childhood.

Babies and children between birth and 3 have never before been afforded high status in our society, or even viewed as separate entities from their mothers, whilst, in full daycare, they have until very recently been considered the subject of care, rather than education. However, Elinor Goldschmied, an expert in childcare practice, refers to 'people under three', rather than 'children' when she discusses the age group (1994). This highlights a further premise on which this chapter is based, that young children are individuals from the time they are born, and that what happens to them at every moment is important, since their lives are not simply seen as a process of becoming, but in a state of 'being' in the present, so that 'the child is conceived of as a person' (James et al. 1998: 207).

We know that, whilst babies are completely dependent on adults from birth, to have their primary needs met, they are also active learners who are equipped to communicate, are able to imitate others, thereby indicating that they have a rudimentary sense of self, and that they can contribute to relationships. They also strive to become independent and are intensely curious, finding out about the world through all of their senses. Early childhood is a period of extremes in which children move from total dependence to relative independence, from reflexive movements to intentional movements, and from communicating non-verbally to communicating verbally. However, the basis of this transition is seen to lie in effective early relationships upon which babies and young children are able to premise future relationships, storing the first of these as internal working models of how relationships work.

Developing a sense of self as a person is another major task of early childhood, when babies and young children begin to build up a mental model of themselves as separate from others. This emerging sense of self is enhanced or reduced by the feedback the young child receives from those around them, and the way they come to view themselves as either loveable or unloveable. For children in daycare this process can be somewhat fragmented, unless the adults involved with the child strive to ensure consistency of care between a small number of people, such as the main carer at home and a key person in the daycare setting. Failure to maintain effective relationships can affect children's development, particularly their emotional development, since a 'baby's stable, and secure relationship with his caregiver is essential to normal brain development. [and] Continued elevated stress hormones such as cortisol can be hazardous to the brain' (Eliot 1999; Schore 1999).

Like childhood, the notion of child development is a difficult concept, since it is mainly a Minority World preoccupation and its discourses arguably maintain the status quo. Indeed, developmental psychology has been described as having 'firmly colonized childhood in a pact with medicine, education and government agencies' (James et al. 1998: 17). Its claims are strongly contested by critical psychology of development proponents, who argue that 'developmental statements will always hinder rather than help', since 'the "facts" about development are subject to constant revision', and that there is no consensus about which 'forms of knowledge or processing capacity, should be thought of as inborn' (Morss 1996: 157). However, research in neuroscience and the mapping of the genome, together with improved scanning technologies, continue to reveal more and more information about the role of 'nature', and by default nurture, in human development. Indeed, Silven tells us 'there is virtually no aspect of human behaviour that can be called purely genetic', since 'genes interact with their environment at all levels including the molecular' (2002: 349). However, to underestimate the arguments against development, as a reified entity, subject to the complex and detailed scales and measures with which it arms itself, would be both unwise and simplistic. The resolution to this dilemma seemed to us to lie in the social context approach, which argues that development cannot be separated from the context in which it takes place, a belief that has been fundamental to the thinking of the team as we considered the diversity of experiences to which children are subject. Consistent with, and informing, this view is Vygotsky's theory, which posits that 'a child's development cannot be understood unless we examine the external social world in which that individual lives' (Harvard 1996: 39).

In consequence, it was agreed that the childhood we were concerned with was as much a temporal as a cultural construct, relevant to an age of technological change, shaped by an increasing emphasis on individuals rather than community, and one of uncertainty, in which anxiety about children's safety is rife. It seemed also that in a period when knowledge about young children is expanding, this should be reflected in any materials. Finally, child development was seen as both a help and a hindrance in describing the way children grow and develop and it was recognized that since all knowledge is contingent upon future findings there is still much uncertainty about human development. We were nonetheless aware that this problem must be reconciled in a satisfactory way.

As a society we have become very interested in babies and young children, yet research on childcare and young children is a fairly new area. Traditionally, the word 'research' has been associated with experiments, laboratory conditions and statistics, though more recently this approach has been challenged by a more personal approach, reflected in the words associated with practitioner research such as participant observation, anecdotal records, diary entries and reflection on practice.

Research matters

The dilemma for us, for whom research is important, was that having been invited to undertake this task, because of our considered expertise in the field, the necessity for undertaking any further research could have been precluded. However, the development of a framework to influence and support practitioners in their day-to-day work with babies and young children required that the views, expectations and involvement of this group must be a priority from the outset. This necessitated that there should be considerable consultation with a number of interest groups, and, although practitioners were represented on the Steering and Working Groups, it was important that the views of as wide a range of practitioners as possible should be sought and used to inform the thinking behind the emerging Framework.

In determining the approach to be taken, the conclusion reached was that since 'Research is best conceived as the process of arriving at dependable solutions to problems through the planned and systematic collection, analysis and interpretation of data' (Mouly 1978: 12), the research method adopted was to be a combination of both quantitative and qualitative methods, with an emphasis on accessing 'real-life' evidence. Derived from a mix of methodologies, this included a combination of face-to-face and telephone interviews, focus group debate, participant and non-participant involvement in settings ranging from childminders' homes and Sure Start programmes to private day nurseries, Early Excellence Centres and parent programmes. We believed this would provide the breadth of views and opinions required to begin to develop the Framework.

A number of further issues and necessary tasks also faced us. The requirement to produce a review of literature and research and to ensure that relevant findings underpinned the development of the framework was a major commitment in terms of time alone. Professor Tricia David and her team undertook this task.

At the same time it was necessary to identify and review existing 'frameworks', which, although not necessarily developed specifically for the birth to 3 age group, nevertheless would inform the new framework and serve to challenge the thinking of the team. Whilst it could be argued that those reviewed were not frameworks as such, but rather approaches to working with young children based on specific underpinning theory and a guiding philosophy, nevertheless for the purposes of the project they were an extremely useful starting point. The following frameworks/approaches/programmes were reviewed:

- High/Scope, 1979 (Hohmann et al.);
- Reggio Emilia, 1993 (Edwards et al.);
- Te Whariki, New Zealand, 1996 (Ministry of Education);
- Quality in Diversity, Early Childhood Education Forum, 1998 (ECEF);
- Peers Early Education Programme (PEEP), 2001 (Peep Learning Ltd.);
- Sure Start, 2002 (DfES Publications).

Practitioners' views

A number of questions were asked about each approach. These related to the aims of each programme/approach/framework, its underpinning principles, influential theories informing each, ways in which the child was characterized, areas of learning and development emphasized, and ways in which each framework was presented. The information gained was then used to inform thinking in relation to the proposed framework, subsequently named *Birth to Three Matters* (DfES 2002).

In order to elicit the views of a wide range of people, a proforma was drawn up and distributed widely and used to guide discussion in both face-to-face and telephone interviews. Over two thousand proformas were distributed nationally and internationally to practitioners; policy makers; organizations representing children from birth to 3 and the adults who work with them; private and voluntary sector personnel; representatives of different sectors and departments responsible for health, care, education, and the inspection of settings. Responses were also returned in the form of electronic communication, papers and examples of written guidelines. Focus groups, which met on a regular basis with the Project Director, were established regionally. During the consultation stage initial views were sought from these groups, which continued to meet for the duration of the project and were involved in trialling the materials.

The proforma sought responses to the following questions:

1) What would you **not** wish to see in a Framework to support those working with the 0–3 age range?
2) What principles, therefore, do you feel should underpin the proposed Framework?
3) What **would** you like to see in a future Framework?
4) What kind of experiences would you envisage as being appropriate for this age range?
5) What kind of support would you require in order to implement the kind of Framework you envisage?
6) What else needs to be considered when developing this Framework?

The willingness of people to talk with the project team and to share their 'stories' as well as their hopes and intentions for the proposed Framework endorses the view that: 'research produces stories as well as facts and figures' (Blenkin and Kelly 1997: 58). Results from this consultation process revealed a high level of agreement between potential users and those responsible for the development of the Framework. There was unanimous agreement on a number of issues:

- that babies were seen as competent and skilful learners from birth;
- that early interactions with a knowledgeable, sensitive and re-sponsive adult were central in early care and education;
- that curriculum or subject headings, ring binders or anything which suggested a top-down model of early learning should be avoided;
- that child-initiated, play-based activities should be at the heart of the process, promoting healthy social and emotional growth.

Debate continued on such issues as working with parents, the definition of and response to children with special needs and disabilities, and what the Framework should look like.

Aims and principles

The aims of the Framework were more clearly defined during this stage and there was a high measure of agreement between respondents and team members with regard to these. The aims of the Framework are:

- to value and celebrate children, their individuality, efforts and achievements;
- to value and support the adults who live and work with children;
- to provide opportunities for reflection;
- to inform and develop practice;
- to acknowledge there are no easy answers.

Much of the literature in the field of early childhood education identifies principles that should underpin any work with young children and families; many of the proponents of these principles were involved in the development of the Framework. It is not surprising, then, that the principles adopted echo those to be found in much of the literature of early childhood care and education (Bruce 1987; Pugh 1992).

Reasonable doubts

Following the establishment of the principles underpinning the Framework, we were disturbed by what we will describe as reasonable doubts concerning the wisdom of writing a framework of effective practice, since we knew that whilst this was a landmark victory in terms of the recognition of the importance of the period between birth and 3 years in children's lives, we were also aware that we stood on the edge of history in setting out a national framework for practice in this field. Whilst we address the issue of these reasonable doubts here, we do so only briefly, since each is worthy of further consideration and could be debated at length; indeed we would argue that it is important that these discussions continue to take place.

In spite of a consensus emerging about the aims and principles underpinning the framework, our first reasonable doubt was the fact that in setting down these guidelines we were invading the last unclaimed, private territory of the home, motherhood, indeed of early childhood itself, since, previously, the care and education of this age group has been purely a private affair, between the parent and the carers, whether in a childminder's home, a preschool group, or a full daycare setting. However, in a society that is becoming increasingly concerned with achieving quality and raising standards, together with increasing anxieties about safety and litigation, it is not unexpected that daycare for babies and young children should become ever more prescribed and regulated, and indeed this move has been welcomed by many.

We were also concerned that in setting down a framework of effective practice we were, by default, also saying something about a curriculum for our youngest children, a politically sensitive issue when the curriculum has previously been related mainly to children over 3 years of age and has been described as 'the concepts, knowledge, understanding, attitudes and skills that a child needs to develop' (DES 1990: 9). However, by defining curriculum broadly, 'as all the experiences both planned and unplanned that the child is involved in, including the physical space, resources and the people with whom the child interacts', we effectively altered the meaning of curriculum, defined earlier, and broadened the term to describe all the child's experiences, rather than simply the outcomes for the child's learning. We considered this broader definition to be one to which we could subscribe and with which we were much more comfortable, accepting that the Framework might offer insights into what a curriculum might comprise, in as much as it commented upon the environment, the activities and the interactions within the setting.

A further issue in setting out a framework for effective practice is that, in some way, it redefines what our culture believes about young children and how they develop, and at the same time outlines what is considered to be 'good' practice with this age group – and, although reference has been made to other frameworks, it is essentially a snapshot of a particular view, taken from a limited perspective, not dissimilar to our earlier discussions of childhood. It could also be argued that it assumes a homogeneity of cultural beliefs and practices, which is at best unlikely and at worst mistaken, in a diverse and multicultural society. Taking account of these principles, the way childhood has been variously defined, and the impact of social context on children's experience, while respecting the view of babies and young children as people in their own right, and recognizing the many arguments surrounding approaches to development, we began to address the complex issue of how to characterize the child in the Framework.

Traditionally, development has been described in terms of physical, cognitive, linguistic, emotional and social dimensions, all of which appeared to us to dissect the child's development into separate domains, rather than to reflect in a holistic and multidimensional way real children with personalities, thoughts, emotions, ideas, skills and dispositions. Discussions, research and reading about children led us to view them as whole beings with a sense of self, which in the right conditions would emerge to make them powerful. At the same time, we felt it important to acknowledge the child as being both a learner and a communicator, from birth. Finally, using a broad definition of what constitutes good health, our child was to be thought of as healthy. The child was then described as: A Strong Child, A Skilful Communicator, A Competent Learner and A Healthy Child. One problem with this approach is that, traditionally, childcare courses have presented the study of child development in a simplistic way, detailing milestones which are easily understood and set out the child's expected development in vision, motor movement, language, communication, cognition and social and emotional areas. However, the analysis of the child into such units obscures from view the sentient child who is active in their own development and who is a person in their own right.

A further doubt we encountered was in relation to the introduction of new terminology. We considered that, for someone who has not been inducted into the Framework, the Aspect headings could be confusing, particularly as A Strong Child and A Healthy Child are capable of being interpreted in several ways. So, the introduction of new terminology and new ways of thinking and talking about babies and young children could, we thought initially, create difficulties in terms of language and accessibility. However, it seemed that a positive outcome of representing babies and young children in this way was that we were suggesting new ways in which to talk and think about children, which, in turn, would offer new insights into the ways they were viewed by practitioners, parents, theorists and policy makers. A further benefit of this new approach, we believe, is that it offers a foil for challenging earlier views and attitudes. If babies and young children are viewed as strong, competent at learning, and so on, work with them changes commensurately, and the cry, often heard from the uninitiated, that 'babies are boring', will lose its puissance. So, our hope was that if children come to be understood in terms of the four Aspects of the Framework, previously limiting barriers will be broken down, since children are now described in terms of what they are like and what they can do, contrary to the earlier deficit model.

Indicators of growth and development

Next we considered stages of development and, aware of the pro- and anti-developmentalist arguments, were reluctant to fall into the trap of developmental measures and tables. However, at the same time, we were required to provide indicators of development within the framework. An issue raised by identifying broad developmental areas was that of children who did not fit readily into these categories, whose development might be described as atypical, in as much as they might not be sighted, for example, or they might never use oral language. However, it was felt important to acknowledge that all children, whatever their special needs and differences, do strive to communicate, to move, to explore, to play and that as such the descriptors could be helpful in indicating a 'best fit' for all children, regardless of their chronological age. The broad areas, then, are conveyed in four symbols indicating growth and development. The rationale for each broad area is explained in the descriptors that accompany the symbols shown in Table 1.1.

Links with other initiatives

A further challenge was that the Framework should be consistent with the range of initiatives relating to children in the birth to 3 age group and beyond. As a result, explicit links were made with the *Curriculum Guidance for the Foundation Stage* (QCA 2000), the *National Standards for Full Day Care* (DfES 2001), and the Peers Early Education Programme (PEEP Learning Ltd. 2001) project, whilst implicit links were made with the *Children's National Service Framework* (DoH 2001).

A final issue for us was how to produce a Framework which would be equally useful to the diverse range of practitioners working with children from birth to 3, from childminders in their own homes to staff working in large, well-resourced early years centres. The Framework that finally emerged, *Birth to Three Matters* (DfES 2002), was a multi-media pack of materials containing an A2 poster, an introductory booklet, 16 laminated cards, a video and a CD-ROM. The introductory booklet, *An Introduction to the Framework*, explains the relationship between all the elements and provides information about how the materials are presented and can be used. Table 1.2 shows the

Table 1.1 The four broad areas of development

	Heads Up, Lookers and Communicators (0–8 months) During the first 8 months, **young babies** react to people and situations with their whole bodies. They are also competent in observing and responding to their immediate environment and communicating with those around them.
	Sitters, Standers and Explorers (8–18 months) During the period from 8 to 18 months, **babies**' exploration of the environment becomes more intentional. Increasing mobility and language development enable them to find out and understand more about their world.
	Movers, Shakers and Players (18–24 months) From 18 to 24 months, **young children** begin to show increasing independence and obvious pleasure in moving, communicating and learning through play.
	Walkers, Talkers and Pretenders (24–36 months) From 24 to 36 months, **children's** competence at moving, talking and pretending is more and more evident and they show increasing confidence in themselves and skill in making relationships.

Aspects of the child in bold and the Components from each Aspect running across from left to right.

The 16 cards are colour-coded and each card focuses on one of the Components from any of the four Aspects described in Table 1.2, such as Growing and Developing, taken from A Healthy Child. Each card contains the following sections: **Development Matters**, which alerts practitioners to the ways children may be expected to develop in relation to each component; **Look, Listen, Note,** which suggests things to observe about children's behaviour and responses; **Effective Practice** and **Planning and Resourcing** provide examples of the ways in which adults can plan and organize the

Table 1.2 The Aspects and Components

A Strong Child	Me, Myself and I	Being Acknowledged and Affirmed	Developing Self-assurance	A Sense of Belonging
A Skilful Communicator	Being Together	Finding a Voice	Listening and Responding	Making Meaning
A Competent Learner	Making Connections	Being Imaginative	Being Creative	Representing
A Healthy Child	Emotional Well-being	Growing and Developing	Keeping Safe	Healthy Choices

environment and resources to support a particular component. The reverse side of each card includes information about ways of **Meeting Diverse Needs** and of providing **Play and Practical Support**, together with addressing **Challenges and Dilemmas** faced by some practitioners in their work. Finally, there is a **Case Study** or a series of photographs on each card providing supporting information in the development of each Component.

We have discussed the conceptualization, development and production of the *Birth to Three Matters* Framework (DfES 2002) and have begun the debate about some of the issues raised, including our 'reasonable doubts'. We now envisage these issues being central to any future debates about young children, early childhood care and education, and policy and practice, not only in England, but also within the wider early years community. We believe such debates to be both healthy and necessary, and have valued those in which we have been involved following the publication of the materials. We look forward to many more in the future as the *Birth to Three Matters* Framework continues to guide provision and shape practice for our youngest children.

References

Abbott, L. and Langston, A. (2002a) Birth to Three Matters, *Early Childhood Practice: The Journal for Multi-Professional Partnerships*, Vol. 4(2).

Abbott, L. and Langston, A. (2002b) Looking good, *Nursery World*, Vol. 102(3845), 12 December.

Abbott, L. and Langston, A. (2003a) Strong points, *Nursery World*, Vol. 103(3855), 27 February.

Abbott, L. and Langston, A. (2003b) Birth to Three Matters, first learning, *Nursery Education*, Issue 58, February.

Abbott, L. and Langston, A. (2003c) Talk to me, *Nursery World*, Vol. 103(3859), 27 March.

Abbott, L. and Langston, A. (2003d) In good health, *Nursery World*, Vol. 103(3867), 22 May.

Abbott, L. and Pugh, G. (eds) (1998) *Training to Work in the Early Years: Developing the Climbing Frame*. Buckingham: Open University Press.

Blenkin, G.M. and Kelly, A.V. (1997) *Principles in to Practice in Early Childhood Education*. London: Paul Chapman Publishing.

Bruce, T. (1987) *Early Childhood Education*. London: Paul Chapman Publishing.

DES (1990) *Starting with Quality: Report of the Committee of Inquiry into the Educational Experiences Offered to Three-and-Four Year-Olds (the Rumbold Report)*. London: HMSO.

DfEE (2001) *Schools – Building on Success*. London: DfEE.

DfES (2001) *National Standards for Under Eights Day Care and Childminding*. London: DfES.

DfES (2002) *Birth to Three Matters* (DfES Publications, London).*

DoH (2001) *Children's National Service Framework, CNSF*. London: DoH.

ECEF (1998) *Quality in Diversity in Early Learning: A Framework for Early Childhood Practitioners*. London: ECEF and NCB.

Edwards, C., Ghandini, L. and Forman, G. (eds) (1993) *The Hundred Languages of Children – The Reggio Emilia Approach to Early Childhood Education*. Norwood, NJ: Ablex.

Eliot, L. (1999) *Early Intelligence: How the Brain and Mind Develop in the First Five Years of Life*. London: Penguin.

Goldschmeid, E. and Jackson, S. (1994) *People Under Three*. London: Routledge.

Harvard, G. (1998) The key ideas of Vygotsky and their implications for teaching and schooling, in P. Preece and R. Fox (eds) *Perspectives on Constructivism, Perspectives 56*. Exeter: School of Education, University of Exeter.

Hohmann, M., Banet, B. and Weikart, D. (1979) *Young Children in Action*. London: High/Scope Press.

James, A., Jenks, C. and Prout, A. (1998) *Theorizing Childhood*. Cambridge: Polity Press.

James, A. and Prout, A. (1997) *Constructing and Reconstructing Childhood*. Basingstoke: Falmer Press.

Langston, A. (2003) All about working with under threes, *Nursery World*, Vol. 103(3878), 7 August.

Langston, A. and Abbott, L. (2003) Born to learn, *Nursery World*, Vol. 103(3863), 24 April.

Ministry of Education (1996) *Te Whariki*. Wellington: Learning Media Limited.

Morss, J.R. (1996) *Growing Critical: Alternatives to Developmental Psychology*. London and New York: Routledge.

Mouly, G.J. (1978) *Educational Research: The Art and Science of Investigation*. Boston, MA: Allyn and Bacon.

PEEP Learning Ltd. (2001) *Learning Together Series*. Oxford: PEEP Publications.

Pugh, G. (ed.) (1992) *Contemporary Issues in the Early Years*. London: Paul Chapman Publishing.

QCA (2000) *Curriculum Guidance for the Foundation Stage*. London: QCA.

Qvortrup, J., Bardy, M., Sgritta, G. and Wintersberger, H. (eds) (1994) *Childhood Matters, Social Theory, Practice and Politics*. Aldershot: Avebury.

Schore, A.N. (1999) Foreword, in J. Bowlby *Attachment and Loss*, Vol. 1: Attachment. New York: Basic Books.

Silven, M. (2002) Origins of knowledge: learning and communication in infancy, *Learning and Instruction*, 12: 345–74.

Sure Start (2002) *Making a Difference for Children and Families*. Nottingham: DfES Publications.

*DfES (2002) *Birth to Three Matters* is available in hard copy from Prolog on 0845 60 222 60, or on the World Wide Web at: *www.surestart.gov.uk/*

2　Aspects Matter

Ian Barron and Rachel Holmes

Introduction

Ian Barron and Rachel Holmes are members of the Early Years and Childhood Studies Centre at the Manchester Metropolitan University and were members of the *Birth to Three Matters* Project Team involved in the conception, development and subsequent progression of the Framework. In this chapter they consider the Aspects that describe children as strong, as skilful communicators, competent learners and healthy children.

Aspects matter

Aspects matter because they are the essence of the way in which *Birth to Three Matters* (DfES 2002) characterizes children. In setting out to create the Framework, the team was committed to ensuring that the ways in which children's living, learning and development were conceptualized were consistent with deeply held beliefs about the nature of children and of childhood. Whilst it would have been easy to fall back on curriculum-based notions of children's development or to use the conventional stages outlined in much child development literature, we were concerned to move to a more holistic, socially and culturally situated model.

As noted by James (1999), for much of the twentieth century (and beyond), developmental psychology dominated how children were understood. Stage-based models of development have dominated, with children being seen, too often, as deficient because they had not yet developed all the knowledge, skills and understanding of adults. Before the twentieth century, evangelical views tended to hold sway, with children again being seen as deficient but often because of the doctrine of original sin (see Jenks 1996; James and Prout 1997). The road to 'goodness' was usually seen as needing to be marked with due chastisement. The eighteenth century could be seen to have had a more positive view of children, with the Romantic conception of innocence and of children as having certain powers, portrayed by Rousseau and Wordsworth. This Romantic notion also contained the related construct of children as in need of protection in order to enable development to take its natural course. This Romantic view of children has to some extent found later expression in child-centred views of children's learning and development.

Child-centred views, however, have often been essentially stage-based developmental views, and could be seen to start from the deficit model described earlier. Hence a great deal of time has been spent discussing children's lack of ability and understanding. In part, this reflects Piaget's (1975) view of young children as egocentric. Later, in the wake of Piaget, the discussion moved on to consider how young children displayed social competence earlier than Piaget had claimed, provided that the situations made 'human sense' (Donaldson 1978; Dunn 1988).

The past ten years, however, have seen a questioning of the traditional views of developmental psychology (Burman 1994, 1999; Morss 1996; James 1999); a growth in the influence of sociology in the study of children and childhood; and growing recognition that the way we view children is largely a social and cultural construct. Neuroscience has also made significant advances in studying the brain development of children in their first three years, which has made a significant difference to the way children's competence is now perceived (Shore 1997; Trevarthen 1998; Gopnik et al. 1999; Shonkoff and Phillips 2000).

The views held by the Project Team were influenced by findings from developmental psychology, sociology and neuroscience. The *Birth to Three Matters* Framework (DfES 2002) presents Aspects in which children are viewed as competent at least in particular things in particular contexts (Murray and Andrews 2000). The Aspects are a means of conceptualizing children as they explore and negotiate knowledge, skills and understandings in particular social, institutional and cultural contexts (Harkness and Super 1996).

A Strong Child

Within the context of the Framework, A Strong Child is premised upon a number of ideas that suggest the baby becomes aware of, and confident about, themselves and their relationship in interaction with others and the world around them (Vygotsky 1978). It is suggested that this process is complex, and within the Framework is conceived as four Components, each contributing to, and complementing, the others: Me, Myself and I; Being Acknowledged and Affirmed; Developing Self-Assurance; and A Sense of Belonging. In order to nurture the many ways in which a child is 'strong', it is important that they are given the opportunity to flourish whilst being supported within a secure relationship. Cottone suggests, 'we are born of relationship, nurtured in relationship and educated in relationship' (1988: 363).

Far from this existing as an adult-dominated relationship, in which the adult maintains the power to influence, control and determine, A Strong

Child recognizes that the relationship is reciprocal. From birth, it is ac-knowledged that babies learn they can have influence *upon* and are influenced *by* others. Furthermore, the facilitation of this learning requires recognition and effective responses from adults, by actively listening to, communicating with, and sharing the intricate nuances of each child's interactive experience.

Greenhalgh (1994) proposes that developing an awareness of the com-plex nature of learning about self requires the practitioner to take a broad perspective (see Figure 2.1).

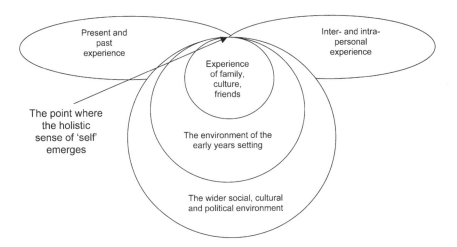

Figure 2.1   Sense of self (adapted from Greenhalgh 1994: 12).

He suggests that there is a web of intricate intra-personal and inter-rela-tional processes that embed each individual child within any particular context. It is through the nature of these inter-relational processes that a child grows to understand who they are and develops a sense of belonging. Ex-pressed within all Components of the Aspect A Strong Child are ways in which these internal and external influences find confluence and manifest themselves in individualistic and holistic ways. Valuing individuality, finding differentiated ways to nurture communication, exploring emotional bound-aries, and recognizing differences and similarities all promote an awareness of the depths of intense experience. These immerse each child in a world of colour, intricately woven with and influenced by the interplay of cultural expectations and the immutability of gender worlds. In relation to these processes, through the advocacy of problematizing practice, this Aspect raises some challenges and dilemmas for contemplation.

The following statement taken from the Component card for Developing Self-Assurance, together with the example of practice offered, raises some interesting dilemmas for practitioners – 'Children's self-confidence is affected and influenced by the way adults respond to them' (DfES 2002). Given that there are vast numbers of 'adults' who respond in very different ways to each child – parent(s)/carer(s), practitioners, other family members, friends of family members and so on – it has to be noted that they will all respond with different beliefs, value systems and specific agendas. Embedded within a cultural and religious framework, a parent may find it inappropriate that their 32-month-old child begins to undress when a group of other children are taking their wet clothes off after being sprayed with water. The practitioner may well regard the child's inclusion in the spontaneous undressing activity as something they clearly want to do, as a valuable part of belonging to the group and experiencing the sensations attached to what would seem like an 'innocent' and pleasurable activity. How do we, as practitioners, resolve what seems to be a conflict of interests? As professionals, do we make judgements about what is in the best 'educational' interests of the child, even if that silences the parent's voice? How do we interpret the parent's agenda; do we stand in judgement of cultural and religious practices that seem to raise questions about the realities of living in a multicultural society? To position this dilemma within Greenhalgh's framework, the genesis is the point at which all these internal and external influences come together – the child. It is important to experience the child in relation to the past and present influences that surround them. A child's predominant sense of identity and belonging will be embedded within their immediate family, rooted within complex cultural, class, religious and racial messages. Layered within this are a plethora of societal and political messages, some of which emerge from, and are communicated through, the media. Woven through this seemingly dichotomous context, borne out of the political and societal agendas in which it is embedded, but striving to be representative of the local community it serves, is the institution of the early years setting, where the need to be 'politically correct' may well inhibit a practitioner's beliefs about how young children 'should' be cared for and educated. It is at the interface of these and other complex dilemmas that this Aspect positions the practitioner. Whose definition of a 'strong' child do we mean? Whose do we use? Whose do we perceive as the absolute in educational terms?

Reinforcing a child's sense of individuality whilst also nurturing a sense of group belonging emerges from the recognition that each child is a member of a family and a community, rather than an isolated individual. It is therefore regarded as central to A Strong Child that any setting is seen as a system of relations embedded in a wider social system within which the child operates, finds meaning, and develops a sense of individual and group identity. Developing a sense of belonging is underpinned by an appreciation of the ways in which family, culture and setting are pivotal to an active partnership in a child's developing self-awareness and self-knowing. Exchanges of ideas and sharing of different wisdoms deem parents as quintessential co-contributors to the child's holistic and individualistic learning experience. Threads of this appreciation can be seen throughout this Aspect. The Component card A Sense of Belonging reinforces this point: 'the recognition of the significance of each child's race, culture, ability and gender comes from the respect for, and value of, difference' (DfES 2002).

Presenting A Strong Child creates many questions and re-directs the practitioner to areas for contemplation, re-evaluation and re-conceptualization. These include:

- the nature of the provision made for nurturing self-confidence;
- the parent's role in building a strong sense of cultural belonging;
- the practitioner's role in preserving and building on the child's sense of individuality;
- how the child is viewed and valued in relationship with others; and
- how the practitioner views the holistic nature of the process of learning about self.

By beginning to realize they are separate and different from others, the young child makes 'new connections', by seeing themselves through others and in the construction and reconstruction of their own ideas in relation to others (Raney and Hollands 2000). Salmon writes 'understanding does not proceed quantitatively, by a series of additive steps, but by significant changes of position, of angle of approach, changes in the whole perspective from which everything is viewed' (1988: 79).

A Strong Child advocates the practitioner focusing upon how children explore, play, socialize and make sense of their experiences, which suggests that these behaviours change, evolve, shift and develop as the child reconstructs, re-conceptualizes and re-evaluates their perceptions and understandings of themselves in relation to others and the wider world. This Aspect acknowledges that this is a process whereby the recognition of personal characteristics, preferences and understandings about self, identity and belonging are shaped and defined in relationship with others.

A Skilful Communicator

Communication is multifaceted and sophisticated and central to what it means to be human. Birth to 3 does indeed matter, but in becoming a skilful communicator, as in much else, communication seems to begin before birth. The ways in which mother and baby communicate *in utero* become the basis for much of the communication that follows (Karmiloff and Karmiloff-Smith 2001). Only forty or so years ago it was believed that babies were incapable of feeling and capable of very little in the way of communication. Now it is much better understood that babies are socially communicative beings from birth (and perhaps before).

Both Vygotsky (1962) and Bruner (1983) point to the significance of communication and language, first as a way of ensuring that the child's needs are met and, later, as a means of organizing thought. They also draw our attention to the ways in which all learning is essentially social in nature. Communication and language, therefore, develop in the social processes of what it means to be together. From moments after birth, babies have a preference for the human face, so essential in beginning to communicate with others. Very soon, they also have a preference for the human voice over other sounds and for familiar voices over unfamiliar ones (Murray and Andrews 2000). They respond with sounds, with gestures and with movements to what is said to them. It does matter, however, as Goldschmied and Selleck (1996) point out, that they are together with significant people who give them close attention in terms of facial expression, actions, gestures and language. Without the closeness of 'being together' babies will not have the opportunity to develop and fine tune their communicative skills.

Significant adults behave in ways that signal to the baby their attention to them. This takes the form of touch, gesture, facial expression and modulation of the voice. Babies quickly learn that communication is a two-way process and it is not only the baby that responds to the adult, the adult also responds to communication from the baby, and so the interactive, synchronous relationship that is at the heart of effective communication begins to develop. Sensitive, effective adults see babies as communicators and in so doing give meaning to the babies' communication. They respond in ways that seek to make meanings as clear as possible to the child, using language patterns often referred to as 'motherese', and make a great deal of use of rhyme and associated action (Buckley 2003). In so doing, babies come to learn that certain sorts of communicative acts, on their part, will elicit responses from adults. Babies come to learn that these responses lead to their needs being met and bring enjoyment and pleasure. Thus, the beginnings of turn-taking appear as the essential basis for two-way communication.

Therefore, language develops in the social context of 'getting things done' (Dunn 1988). In playing, feeding, bathing and changing, caregivers talk to babies in the expectation that they will understand. Babies 'listen' carefully to what is said to them and, drawing on the full range of cues available to them and looking carefully at gestures made by familiar adults in familiar contexts, they start to 'respond' in seemingly contingent ways. In turn, sensitive and tuned-in caregivers also search for the baby's meaning and respond in ways that demonstrate that it was worthwhile finding a voice. The better tuned the adult to the baby's attempts at communicating, the more the baby's voice will be heard. The more caregiver and child share, explore and inhabit each other's worlds, the sooner first words are likely to appear, which are then clarified, repeated and echoed by the adult. In getting things done and in ensuring that needs and opinions are expressed these single words begin to be used in two- and three-word combinations (often referred to as 'telegraphic speech') that contain the bare essence of the message as young children become increasingly skilled in 'making meaning'.

Meaning-making, too, is a social process. The child's initial attempts at making meaning in the world are, as we have seen, very much concerned with ensuring that needs are met. Children seek to make sense of their experiences of themselves, of significant adults and of their siblings. They seek to make sense of a family world where there are things to done and battles to be won. Increasing language competence enables them to begin to ask questions about themselves, their families and about the world around them. As they make meanings for themselves, they seek to apply these meanings to others.

> Liam, two months short of his third birthday, was staying with his family in a Lancashire hotel where references to the legends of witches who inhabit Pendle Hill were strong, with life-sized models of witches everywhere. He asked questions about what the models were and why they were there. As his grandfather approached one, Liam shouted 'Come away, granddad – it might frighten you'.

Liam's meanings, understanding and concern for his grandfather (and himself!) all find expression in just a few words.

Making sense of the world and making meaning are the essence of the processes of development in the work of Piaget (1975), Vygotsky (1962, 1978) and Bruner (1986, 1990). Whether the concern is with understanding the self, others, the world around us, language or literacy, the same principles are seen to be at work. Thus, not only are children seen as making sense and meaning about language from birth, but they are making sense of literacy too. The sense that they make of literacy will, as Heath (1983) has helped us to understand, depend on the particular niche where the sense is being made, because literacy is experienced differently in different cultures and in different homes. How children go about this process of making sense of literacy has resonance with the way that they begin to make sense of spoken language: they look at pictures, they consider the situations that are depicted in them, they encourage adults to help them, they express the meanings that they are making and seek feedback from adults, who duly provide it; they show interest in rhyming and other words. They learn to recognize words like 'crocodile' and 'hippopotamus' by their shape, long before they learn to read and understand words such as 'the' and 'and'. They begin to experiment with their own mark-making in pictures and words (Bissex 1980). They imitate the appearance of writing, they start to record its key features as they begin to understand the alphabetic system, using writing that has many of the qualities of telegraphic speech (Ferreiro and Teberosky 1983). All of this meaning-making depends, however, on appropriate support from adults who can help children in their discoveries. As Vygotsky (1962) helps us to understand, making sense of literacy is more difficult than making sense of language because, as a symbolic system, it is one step further removed: there are no gestures or contextual cues to draw upon and the creator of the literate text is not likely to be present to answer questions or to provide additional support. Making sense of literacy is also best conceived of as a social act in which a child and an adult in a particular culture seek to make sense of the conventions of print. This is particularly in evidence in the *Birth to Three Matters* video (DfES 2002), in which a childminder with a baby and young girl explore together the meaning and sense of language in a way that is enjoyable.

A Competent Learner

This Aspect is concerned with understanding how babies and young children develop as competent learners. Learning is conceived of as being made up of four main elements, or Components. These are concerned with Making Connections, Being Imaginative, Being Creative and Representing. These elements are all heavily interconnected, particularly by the way in which they all involve children in exploring, experimenting and interacting as they seek to learn about the world around them in a variety of ways.

Competent learners are seen as having considerable competence in ensuring that their particular needs are met. They are finely tuned into the world around them and, given appropriate and contingent support from adults and other children, they will make the most of an environment that provides them with interesting materials and equipment, one that appeals to the senses and which encourages movement. They will do this best in the company of sensitive and responsive adults and other children who will enable them to make sense of what they have experienced. Babies and young children are seen as needing to be able to learn the things that they want to learn, when given sufficient time and encouraged to make choices. Finally, they need opportunities to communicate, share and represent their learning in a variety of forms, including through the imagination, through creative responses and through mark-making.

Babies and young children are naturally curious and they start to learn and to understand the world around them through the sensory and physical exploration that they engage in and enjoy. These explorations are playful but they are also deeply meaningful, and babies and young children have a deeply rooted desire to interpret and to understand the world around them. That this exploration is physical and sensory, however, is not to deny the significance of the relationship between physical action and brain development in the youngest children. As noted by Shore (1997), babies' perceptive abilities and their brains predispose them to make sense of the world around them.

In this conception of the Competent Learner a connection runs deep between experience and the way in which the brain is formed. As babies explore the world using touch, sight, sound, taste, smell and movement, so these sensory and physical explorations affect the patterns that are laid down in the brain. Through repeated experience of people, objects and materials, young children begin to form mental pictures that represent them. These mental images then enable the child to increasingly make sense of new experiences by reference to ones already encountered. This is a useful and powerful way of learning about the world because it means that young children can classify and begin to make sense of their world, and these classifications become a reference point for trying to understand new experiences.

Terrence is 33 months old and has just arrived in a new district and new early years setting. From the outset, he expressed a real fascination with sticky tape, masking tape, in fact any adhesive tape that he could wrap around himself and objects. The practitioner responded by providing him with copious amounts of tape in different colours, thicknesses, a range of textures and a pair of scissors and sat with him throughout, as he pondered and explored the possibilities. Terrence spent almost an hour and a half meticulously repeating patterns, wrapping tape around a chair, around the four legs, the seat, the back and then enveloping the sitting space with a tent-like structure that connected the seat with the back. His deliberated gestures suggested he was mapping out where the next piece of tape would be placed and the effort applied to carefully cutting smaller pieces to fill in gaps was astonishing. He didn't say anything as he worked on his chair, but did take time to move around the object, viewing it from different perspectives and looking for gaps. When his explorations came to an end, he said 'There!' as he walked away. Terrence was clearly 'connecting ideas and understanding the world' (DfES 2002) as he communicated the connections he was making, both physically and in terms of developing schema.

Even as young as one month of age, babies are organizing their perceptions and linking them with previous experiences of people and events (Bruce and Meggitt 2002: 92). Piaget calls these early concepts schema. As these mental images and patterns of understanding are laid down in the brain, so 'connections' begin to be formed between them. As Shore (1997), Catherwood (1999) and Shonkoff and Phillips (2000) note, the richness of experiences at this stage is very important to the development and strengthening of synapses in the brain. Where synapses are not fed and strengthened by experience, they will wither and be eliminated, the connections lost, at least temporarily. However, rich experiences enable connections to be made, and so the child comes to make increasing sense of the world.

Whilst young children are naturally curious and keen to make sense of and to represent the world for themselves, they are, as Vygotsky (1978) in particular has helped us to understand, also intensely social. This sociability suggests children are not as egocentric as Piaget claimed. Dunn (1988) has done much to help us to understand that they inhabit a social world in which children learn (at least in varying degrees in different contexts) that there is advantage in seeing the world from another's point of view, particularly if it ensures that others are outwitted!

In essence, children learn about their world and their culture through interactions with significant adults and other children. Whilst it is clear that children create their own understandings about the world and how it works, they are not making these discoveries entirely alone and what they discover will depend on the help they are given and the experiences that they have. Competent learners are learners who are supported by encouraging and sensitive adults who make very careful decisions about the things that children can do and can learn for themselves, and the things with which they need some help, much in the way that Bruner (1977) conceptualizes 'scaffolding'. More than that, competent learners require skilled adults who know when children need help and how much they need: too much and the child will not learn from and take control of the experience, too little and the experience will be frustrating and a possible source of failure.

As young children become more mobile, able to control motor movements, to form mental images of actions, events and experiences, and to understand how one thing can stand for another, so their explorations become far more intentional. As Duffy notes 'children need to represent their experiences, their feelings and ideas if they are to preserve them and share them with others' (1998: 9).

Young children remain intensely active and physical, however, and early mark-making and creative activity may record what the body will do and record the child's exhilaration in physical activity. As Matthews (2002) notes, marks may not remain on the paper at this stage if the arm is swinging enthusiastically around the body and if the paper is small. This physical and sensory exploration of objects and materials will, however, lead young children to begin to represent their experiences of the world around them using whatever materials are to hand. They will experiment, imitate, play with objects and materials, organize and classify, and use marks of different sorts to represent their physical explorations. These early forms of representation demonstrate that children understand how one thing can be used to stand for another. It is important also to note that creativity is not just about the representation of physical actions or the outward expression of a developing mind. It involves the emotions too and, as Malaguzzi suggests, 'creativity requires that the school of knowing finds connections with the school of expressing, opening the doors to the hundred languages of children' (1998: 77).

Early forms of representation can also demonstrate children's interest in particular schema, as they explore their significance as a tool for making sense of certain things in the world around them. As Athey (1990) has helped us to understand, children may become interested in vertical and straight lines, circles, the way that one object can cover another, the way that one thing can be inside another but still visible. These interests and concerns may be represented in physical and 'imaginative' activities, as children run in lines and circles, and cover the tea set with a blanket, but they will also appear in their painting, drawing and mark-making.

Mark-making will record the body's actions, but it will also record what things look like and what things do (see Clay 1975; Temple et al. 1992; McGee and Richgels 1999). It will record the swirl of the helicopter blades, the swerving of the car and the bouncing rain. Eventually, children come to see that the printed word represents people, ideas and words in ways that are not to do with what they look like or what they do, but not before they have experimented with all these possibilities, in the richness of a multimodal discourse that combines numerous ways of 'representing', in the manner described by Kress and Van Leeuwen (2001).

In this multimodal dance, making connections, creativity, imagination and representation begin to mean that children can share their thoughts, feelings, understandings and identities with others using drawings, words, movement, music, and imaginative play. As the Competent Learner approaches the Foundation Stage and beyond, Duffy notes (1998: 9) that from these forms of representation 'springs the understanding to comprehend other forms of symbolic representation, such as written language and mathematics'.

A Healthy Child

Within the Aspect A Healthy Child, the term 'health' is understood as generic and holistic (Meggitt 2001), representing a combination of fluid dynamics including:

- physical health;
- psychological well-being;
- growth and development;
- safety and protection from harm; and
- ways children learn to make healthy choices in their lives.

Each of these areas could be deconstructed as a discrete contributor to a child's health, but within this Aspect they are referred to in relationship with one another, with any one having the potential to influence and impact on others. The importance of developing secure relationships for the child is again woven into the fabric of this Aspect, particularly the notion of enabling a baby to have a close relationship with at least one special person. Developing emotional stability and resilience are expressed as fundamental objectives, which would allow the child to develop confidence in their own, individualized forms of self-expression, healthy dependence and secure independence. Miller (1984) suggests that the 'drama' of being a child is wrought with potential difficulties, largely emerging from the intricacies of their relationships with adults, whose understanding of the child's needs is weakened by being subsumed in their own insecure or unmet emotional needs. The Component card 'Emotional Well-being' points out that 'When a child's independence is developing, they may reject offers of help. Try not to see this as personal rejection but as progress' (DfES 2002). Miller warns that, as adults, the tendency to be absorbed in our own immediate concerns can obscure the emotional realities of the child and so preclude any real sense of being fully receptive to the child's subtle and often symbolic emotional cues or signifiers. The Component 'Emotional Well-being' encourages the practitioner to find sensitive and responsive ways to be engaged with the child, which can facilitate their feeling secure within a relationship that is increasingly predictable. The Component card points out that 'When young children have a close relationship with a caring and responsive adult, they explore from a safe place to which they can return' (DfES 2002). This can suggest a psychological, emotional or physical 'safe place': 'Physical care and loving attention is required in different ways as a toddler becomes mobile ... exploratory behaviour ... takes the child away as she crawls, walks and inspects the world around her' (Selleck and Griffin 1996: 157). Allowing a baby to feel emotionally heard, contained and responded to can enable 'healthy' dependence that nurtures their sustained affective growth; their confidence to find and utilize different forms of affective expression. Having the opportunity to develop a sense of independence that is not enforced, borne out of defence mechanisms, nor a reaction to inattentive practices can foster the emergence of the child who is able to move beyond emotional boundaries, exploring their capabilities and realizing their potential.

Developing a sense of independence builds upon the construction of the child as deeply competent and as an active agent in their own meaning-making, the choices they make and their ongoing learning experiences. The sustained growth and development of the child underpins these notions. By being well nourished, active, rested and protected, by gaining increasing control of their body and acquiring adept physical skills, the young child is supported through a journey of discovery, tentative endeavours, exploration

of the unfamiliar and moments of exhilaration as they accomplish, seek solutions and find reconciliation with their current limitations. Within the
Component Growing and Developing is the idea that a world of energy en-
capsulates the young child, who finds confidence and enthusiasm to explore
the treasures and fantasies that surround them. It is suggested that this world
needs to be juxtaposed with the appreciation of quietness and relaxation,
where they are encouraged to enjoy psychological space in order to develop a
sense of tranquillity and serenity. This balance of activity and contemplation
offers equilibrium within a world where pace, intensity and gravitas engage a
child in a whirlwind of physical and emotional experience.

Being safe and protected implicates the role of the adult in being able to
directly or indirectly facilitate this, by providing an environment and ethos
where the child is encouraged to discover boundaries and limits, learn about
rules, know when and how to ask for help, learn to say no and anticipate
when others will do so (A Healthy Child: Keeping Safe). When considering
the nuances of an environment that is conducive to all aspects of safety, 'it is
counter-productive to focus on keeping children away from every risk,
however slight' (Lindon 1998: 5). This clearly suggests the importance of
knowing the child, their history, capabilities and areas for potential development, so as to assess the degree of risk and how confidently they might
respond to activities. The Component card Keeping Safe notes that 'Children
who have limited opportunity to play, particularly outdoors, may lack a sense
of danger' (DfES 2002). The following scenario creates some interesting
challenges for practitioners, as they wrestle with the intricate balance of
keeping a child safe without resorting to over-protectiveness and for the
child, a sense of being emotionally and physically restrained.

> Chloe is 23 months old. She is an enthusiastic climber, roller, jumper, crawler and
> runner, and given any opportunity will dash for the climbing frame and clamber to
> the top without recourse to any adult support or intervention. Within the past three
> months, she has become much more physically adept, with a greater sense of gross
> motor control and agility, and with these new capabilities she is a whirlwind of
> physical activity, showing no signs of inhibition or fear.

In this scenario, the practitioner is fully aware of the enjoyment that
Chloe experiences as she climbs, manoeuvres and swings from the climbing
frame, but is also conscious that she does not demonstrate any notion of
potential danger as she takes risks that move her beyond what the practitioner believes to be Chloe's physical limitations. Chloe could be perceived as
a child who requires the space, freedom and time to explore and develop her
body and its capabilities, to discover her physical limits by pushing boundaries and taking risks. Alternatively, she could be construed as being

insufficiently aware of danger, in which case it could be considered negligent of the practitioner to allow her this degree of unrestricted exploration without creating tighter physical boundaries. Chloe could be described as independent, but the nuances of whether this is healthy or unhealthy, productive or counter-productive, whether she is safe or at risk, lie embedded within the practitioner's knowledge and understanding of the child. Furthermore, how best to support Chloe in her endeavours to become confidently and independently capable, whilst alert to the dangers inherent within the context she so energetically explores, is a dilemma for the practitioner to contemplate. This practical example can also be used to exemplify the ways in which Chloe is learning to make healthy choices in her life. She clearly enjoyed the experience of climbing, of height, of movement and made specific choices about how she engaged in this. The dilemma presented to the practitioner relates to balancing the importance of mobility within this particular activity to Chloe, with concerns around safety measures that would ensure Chloe was able to develop a fuller understanding of potential dangers and subsequently make 'healthy choices' about what she did and how she did it.

Conclusion

We claimed at the beginning of this chapter that 'Aspects matter' and have demonstrated throughout that each Aspect matters equally if a child is to develop holistically as a strong, skilful, competent and healthy learner and communicator.

References

Athey, C. (1990) *Extending Thought in Young Children*. London: Paul Chapman.

Bissex, G. (1980) *Gnys at Wrk*. Cambridge, Mass.: Harvard University Press.

Bronfenbrenner, U. (1979) *The Ecology of Human Development: Experiments by Nature and Design*. Cambridge, Mass.: Harvard University Press.

Bruce, T. and Meggitt, C. (2002) *Child Care and Education*, 3rd edn. London: Hodder and Stoughton, p. 92.

Bruner, J.S. (1977) *The Process of Instruction*. Cambridge, Mass.: Harvard University Press.

Bruner, J.S. (1983) *Children's Talk: Learning to Use Language*. Oxford: Oxford University Press.

Bruner, J.S. (1986) *Actual Minds, Possible Worlds*. Cambridge, Mass.: Harvard University Press.

Bruner, J.S. (1990) *Acts of Meaning*. Cambridge, Mass.: Harvard University Press.

Buckley, B. (2003) *Children's Communication Skills*. London: Routledge.

Burman, E. (1994) *Deconstructing Developmental Psychology*. London: Routledge.

Burman, E. (1999) Morality and the goals of development, in M. Woodhead, D. Faulkner and K. Littleton (eds) *Making Sense of Social Development*. London: Routledge.

Catherwood, D. (1999) New views on the young brain, *Contemporary Issues in Early Childhood*, Vol. 1 (1): 23–35.

Clay, M. (1975) *What Did I Write?* London: Heinemann.

Cottone, R.R. (1988) Epistemological and ontological issues in counselling: implications of social systems theory. *Counselling Psychology Quarterly*, 1(4): 357–65.

Donaldson, M. (1978) *Children's Minds*. London: Fontana.

Duffy, B. (1998) *Creativity and Imagination in the Early Years*. Buckingham: Open University Press.

Dunn, J. (1988) *The Beginnings of Social Understanding*. Oxford: Blackwell.

Faulkner, D. and Littleton, K. (eds) (1999) *Making Sense of Social Development*. London: Routledge.

Ferreiro, E. and Teberosky, A. (1983) *Literacy Before Schooling*. London: Heinemann.

Goldschmied, E. and Selleck, D. (1996) *Communication Between Babies in their First Year*. London: National Children's Bureau.

Gopnik, A., Meltzoff, A. and Kuhl, P. (1999) *How Babies Think: The Science of Childhood*. London: Weidenfeld and Nicolson.

Greenhalgh, P. (1994) *Emotional Growth and Learning*. London: Routledge.

Harkness, S. and Super, C. (1996) *Parents' Cultural Belief Systems*. New York and London: Guilford Press.

Heath, S.B. (1983) *Ways with Words*. Cambridge: Cambridge University Press.

James, A. (1999) Researching children's social competence, in M. Woodhead, D. Faulkner and K. Littleton (eds) *Making Sense of Social Development (Child Development in Families, Schools and Societies)*. London: Routledge Falmer.

James, A. and Prout, A. (1997) *Constructing and Reconstructing Childhood*, 2nd edn. London: Falmer.

Jenks, C. (1996) *Childhood*. London: Routledge.

Karmiloff, K. and Karmiloff-Smith, A. (2001) *Pathways to Language: From Foetus to Adolescent*. Cambridge, Mass.: Harvard University Press.

Kress, G. and Van Leeuwen, T. (2001) *Multimodal Discourse*. London: Arnold.

Lindon, J. (1998) *Understanding Child Development*. London: Thomson Learning.

Malaguzzi, L. (1998) in C. Edwards, L. Gandini and G. Foreman (eds) *The Hundred Languages of Children*. New York: Ablex.

Matthews, J. (2002) *Developing Drawing and Painting with Young Children*. London: Paul Chapman/Sage.

McGee, L.M. and Richgels, D. (1999) *Literacy's Beginnings*, 3rd edn. London: Allyn and Bacon.

Miller, A. (1984) *The Drama of Being a Child*. London: Virago Press.

Morss, J. (1996) *Growing Critical: Alternatives to Developmental Psychology*. London: Routledge.

Murray, L. and Andrews, E. (2000) *The Social Baby*. London: Richmond Press.

Piaget, J. (1975) *The Child's Conception of the World*. Littlefield: Adams Quality Paperbacks.

Raney, K. and Hollands, H. (2000) Art education and talk – from modernist silence to postmodern chatter, in J. Sefton-Green and R. Sinker (eds) *Evaluating Creativity – Making and Learning by Young People*. London: Routledge.

Shaffer, R. (1996) *Social Development*. Oxford: Blackwell.

Shonkoff, J. and Phillips, D. (2000) *From Neurons to Neighborhoods: The Science of Early Childhood Development*. Washington: National Academy Press.

Shore, R. (1997) *Rethinking the Brain: New Insights into Early Development*. New York: Families and Work Institute.

Temple, C., Nathan, R., Temple, F. and Burris, N. (1992) *The Beginnings of Writing*. London: Prentice Hall.

Trevarthen, C. (1998) The child's need to learn a culture, in M. Woodhead, D. Faulkner and K. Littleton (eds) *Cultural Worlds of Early Childhood*. London: Routledge.

Vygotsky, L.S. (1962) *Thought and Language*. Cambridge, Mass.: MIT Press.

Vygotsky, L.S. (1978) *Mind in Society*. London: Harvard University Press.

3   Policy Matters

Gillian Pugh

Introduction

Since her time as Head of the Early Childhood Unit at the National Children's Bureau to the present, in her current role as Chief Executive of Coram Family and skilled Chair of the Steering Group for the *Birth to Three Matters* project, Gillian Pugh has been centrally involved in many early years initiatives and developments.

She has played significant roles as adviser and consultant to government departments, funding agencies and private and voluntary sector organizations in the development of quality services for young children and their families. She is the first port of call when advice is needed and is held in high esteem by policy makers and practitioners alike.

The early years community owes her a great deal and respects the knowledge, skill and insight that she brings to her work. In this chapter, as well as providing an overview of policy issues, she asserts that policy matters.

Since 'New Labour' came into office in May 1997, services for children and families have been higher on the national agenda than at any time in living memory. Whilst there have been few policies that have focused specifically on children aged birth to 3, there has been a raft of policies aimed at improving services more generally for young children (sometimes because of the value of these services to children themselves, sometimes in order to support women wishing to return to work) and a growing understanding too of the need for support for parents in bringing up their children. Many of these policy initiatives have been informed by research. This chapter summarizes the key policy issues for children aged birth to 3 within the wider context of the agenda for children and families, taking account of some of the research findings that have informed this agenda, and looks briefly at those areas in which policy is still weak.

The government agenda for children and families

Looking at the government's broad policy agenda for children, it is possible to detect some key themes. Those that are of particular relevance to children from birth to 3 are discussed more fully later in the chapter.

1. **Reducing child poverty**. The target set in 1999 was to eradicate child poverty in 20 years and halve it in 10, through additional financial support for all families, and targeted benefits for those most in need. The reduction of poverty is absolutely key to achieving improvements in other areas. The strong association between poverty and poor physical and mental health, low educational attainment, behavioural difficulties, truancy and criminal activity has been proved through numerous studies.

2. **Improving support for families**. The Green Paper *Supporting Families* (Home Office 1998) outlined policies in this area. It was based on children's need for stability and security, and on the government's role in supporting parents to support their children. The Paper included proposals on:

   - access to support (through the establishment of schemes such as Sure Start);
   - better financial support, through increasing child benefit, and through what is now the Child Tax Credit;
   - helping families balance work and home, with improvements in parental leave and pressure on employers to provide more flexible working arrangements for their staff;
   - strengthening marriage;
   - better support for serious problems.

   The role of parents was highlighted again in the Green Paper *Every Child Matters* (HM Treasury 2003) as being integral to any discussion of children's well-being. A new £25,000,000 fund for a National Framework for Parenting Support has been set up, although there is some concern at the strong emphasis within the government's support of parenting programmes on punishing parents for their children's misbehaviour.

3. **Strengthening communities** through local neighbourhood renewal strategies, and through many of the child- and family-centred programmes noted below.

4. **Reducing social exclusion**, a focus on the regeneration of inner-city areas, truancy, homelessness and teenage pregnancy. The 2002

spending review included a cross-cutting review of children at risk which led to an even stronger emphasis on prevention, and the requirement on all local authorities to establish preventive strategies by autumn 2003. In the event, this was overtaken by the emphasis on prevention throughout the paper *Every Child Matters* (HM Treasury 2003).

5. **Improving health**. This is primarily to be achieved through the implementation of *The NHS Plan* (Department of Health 2000). In relation to children this has included setting up a Children's Taskforce with a remit to create a National Service Framework for Children, and linking into other policy initiatives such as Quality Protects, child and adolescent mental health services, adoption, and facilities for children with disabilities.

6. **Raising education standards**, through expanding nursery education, through reducing class sizes, and through introducing standards for literacy and numeracy.

7. **Improving access to work**. This is seen as a key plank in the anti-poverty strategy, and is a fundamental driver behind the expansion of childcare provision as a means of enabling more parents to return to work.

8. **Basing services on**:
   a. **What consumers want**, rather than what service providers think they should have;
   b. **Evidence of what works**, with a strong emphasis on the evaluation of new initiatives.

9. **Joined-up thinking and joined-up services**. This has driven all policy development, and is a central focus of the Green Paper *Every Child Matters* (HM Treasury 2003).

10. **Participation of children and young people in decision-making**. Building on the commitment within the 1989 Children Act to promote the best interests of the child and giving children a voice in decisions that affect their lives.

The impact of research on the policy agenda for children from birth to 3

Despite the increasing emphasis within government policy on young children, there is no specific policy on children from birth to 3. However, looking at the range of policy initiatives that impact on young children, many of these can be seen to have particular relevance for children under 3, and many of them have been informed by research.

Over the past decade there has been a greater understanding from research of the factors that can have an adverse effect on children's development, and those protective factors that we know can help to develop the resilience that children will require if they are to thrive. Some of the risk factors relate to the individual child, for example low birth weight, developmental delay, a difficult temperament, low self-esteem; some to the family, for example poor parental physical or mental health, maternal depression, poor parenting (poor supervision, erratic and inconsistent discipline, little involvement with the child), or conflict between parents; and some to the community, for example social isolation, no early education or daycare, poor material circumstances and housing. Papers summarizing this research and exploring the protective factors were brought to the attention of government in 1998 in the discussions that led to the Sure Start initiative being established (see Pugh 1998, 2002; Oliver and Smith 2000; Bynner 2001: 285–301).

I will now pull out, in summary, some of the key issues that have informed policy over the past few years, taking in turn research relating to the needs of young children, to parents and families, and to communities.

With regard to the needs of young children, there has been a growing understanding of the importance of the first five years of life, and in particular the first year of life. Two areas of research have made a notable impact here. Firstly brain research, which has shown not only how quickly the brain is developing in these early months, but how susceptible it is to environmental influences (Blakemore 2000). We now know that environmental stress has a negative effect not only on how the brain develops but how it functions, and this underlies our capacity to make and sustain relationships. And secondly, a re-assessment of attachment theory has led to a recognition of the importance of secure early attachments to consistent, caring and dependable adults as the basis for a secure sense of self, and the ability to make good relationships later in life.

Whilst these two areas of research have had a specific impact on policy for very young children, a wealth of studies that explore how young children learn and that examine the long-term impact of early education have also influenced the policy debate about expanding services for children under 3. Although the longitudinal Effective Provision for Pre-school Education (EPPE) study (Sammons et al. 2002a; Sammons et al. 2002b) has been concerned with children aged 3 and over, the key findings from this study have obvious implications for younger children, such as the importance of the educational environment of the home, the value of well-trained educators and the importance of an appropriately structured, child-centred curriculum. Of particular relevance to policy for children under 3 are the studies which point to the importance of close and consistent relationships between young children and key workers in nursery settings.

Research that shows the critical role that parents play in their children's early learning and development has also had an impact on policy development, as has the growing understanding of the impact on children's development of different styles of parenting. Positive, nurturing relationships between children and parents provide children with a secure foundation for life, and these relationships are more important in terms of outcomes than family structures. There is also evidence that parenting education and support can successfully offer families a range of knowledge, skills and opportunities for sharing experiences, developing self-confidence and discussing approaches towards parenting (see Pugh et al. 1994).

The other area of research that has influenced policy is that which points to the long-term benefits of preventive work with parents and young children, in both human and financial terms. Simple, relatively inexpensive measures, put into effect early, can prevent the need for more complex and costly intervention later on. The research suggests that, wherever possible, this support is best provided within open-access, mainstream services (health centres, nurseries and so on) in the local community rather than in specialist referral services. A review of preventive work with children experiencing a wide range of difficulties found that three key factors were central to their healthy development: the quality of relationships between parents and their children, the social and economic support available to families, and access to high-quality early education (Sinclair, Hearn and Pugh 1997). Studies of early childhood services have also shown that multi-agency responses to families can meet needs in a holistic way, can promote a joint approach to planning and delivering services, and can make the best use of resources. These findings, too, have influenced the current policy agenda.

The National Childcare Strategy

A central plank of the anti-poverty strategy noted above has been to expand the amount of affordable, good-quality and accessible childcare in order to enable parents to return to work. The National Childcare Strategy was launched in May 1998, alongside the Sure Start Programme. Initiatives since it was launched have included:

- the provision of free part-time nursery education for all 3- and 4-year-olds (2.5 hours a day);
- creating new childcare places for 1.6 million children, primarily through pump priming funds to encourage development within the private sector;
- establishing 100 Early Excellence centres (and more recently the establishment of children's centres, to be set up in the 20 per cent most disadvantaged wards);
- establishing 900 neighbourhood nurseries in disadvantaged areas;

- establishing 500 Sure Start local programmes, aiming to reach up to one-third of young children living in poverty;
- the introduction of financial support for childcare through tax credits for low-income families in work. (The childcare component of the Working Tax Credit aims to help employed parents on lower incomes to meet their childcare costs. Parents must be working at least 16 hours a week, and can claim up to 70 per cent of costs to a maximum of £135 (£94.50) for one child and £200 (£140) for two or more children, provided they use eligible childcare);
- the transfer of childcare regulation and inspection to the Office for Standards in Education (OFSTED);
- establishing a home childcarers scheme, to enable families using registered childcare in their own homes to access the child tax credit;
- support for young parents (between 16 and 19) to access childcare through the 'Care to Learn?' scheme.

The National Childcare Strategy represents considerable progress, with an estimated growth from one place in registered childcare for every nine children under 8 in 1997 to one for every five children in 2003 (Day Care Trust 2003). But there are still wide regional variations, the Working Tax Credit is complex to access, and there is an acute shortage of places for children under 3, although as there are no separate statistics kept for children under 3 the size of the shortfall cannot be quantified. Central government has set high targets for local authorities to achieve in terms of new childcare places, but high capital and revenue costs make these targets difficult to meet. The costs of childcare are also still prohibitive for most parents, with a place for a child under 2 in London estimated to be around £250 a week, considerably more than the tax credit brings in. Understandably, expansion has been targeted on the 20 per cent most disadvantaged wards, through initiatives such as neighbourhood nurseries, Sure Start and children's centres, but this will miss many of the most disadvantaged children, as only 54 per cent of poor children live in these areas.

There is also some concern that the emphasis on encouraging women to return to work as part of the poverty reduction agenda may be at odds with the wish of many parents to stay at home with their young babies. Whilst paid maternity leave was extended to 26 weeks in 2003, and two weeks' paid paternity leave was introduced, and parents of children under 6 now have the right to request flexible working from their employers, this is still insufficient to give parents real choice.

Sure Start local programmes and children's centres

The Sure Start initiative has attracted much attention, with its overall aim of improving the health and well-being of families and children under 4, particularly those who are disadvantaged, so that children have greater opportunity to flourish when they go to school. There are now over 500 Sure Start local programmes in the most disadvantaged areas of the UK, providing services for 16 per cent of children under 4, and a third of all children living in poverty. All programmes have been developed by partnerships of local professionals and parents all working towards the same public service agreements:

- improving social and emotional development;
- improving health;
- improving children's ability to learn;
- strengthening families and communities.

Sure Start was set up as a direct result of the government's first cross-cutting spending review of services for children under 8 and in almost every respect built on the advice that those working in the field gave to an initially sceptical Treasury. There was also a long process of consultation, involving huge numbers of people across the country and with different levels of responsibility. And it really was multi-agency, from Cabinet ministers down to grass-roots workers (see Glass 1999: 257–64).

Although a national programme, each scheme is required to develop in response to local need, but to deliver a number of core services, such as outreach and home visiting, support for families, support for play and learning experiences for children, community-based healthcare, and support for children with special needs. Over the past 18 months there has been a much stronger emphasis on the need to provide childcare places, in line with the ambitious targets noted above. There is also a substantial evaluation programme in place, the first report of which pointed to early successes but also the challenges of working in this multi-agency way to reach the most disadvantaged families (Ball 2002). Part of the Sure Start 'approach' was to change the way in which local services were delivered to families, and a recent development has been the 'mainstreaming' of Sure Start in some local authority areas, whereby all services for children under 3 are delivered using the Sure Start approach, with the local council putting in additional resources to make this possible.

Building on the Sure Start model, and on the Early Excellence programme set up in 1997, a new programme of children's centres was announced in 2002, together with an extended role for schools in meeting the broader needs of families. The concept of children's centres, bringing together the education and welfare of young children and providing broadly based support for children and their parents living in disadvantaged areas, is not a new one. Indeed, it is as old as the first nursery schools set up by Robert Owen in Scotland in the 1800s and was certainly key to the work of the McMillan sisters who came to have such an influence on the development of nursery education in England in the early 1900s. Children's centres are intended to serve children and families in disadvantaged communities and provide integrated nursery education and care for young children, support for families (including daycare for children to enable parents to work), child and family health services and support for other services such as childminder networks, out of school clubs and local neighbourhood nurseries. Joined-up services such as these should be ideally placed to meet the needs of children under 3 and their parents, whether for full daycare or for the informal support that many parents of young children need (see Pugh 2003: 23–9).

Birth to Three Matters

A key policy development for very young children is the establishment of a 'foundation stage' in relation to early education, and the publication in 2000 of the widely welcomed *Curriculum Guidance for the Foundation Stage* (QCA/ DfEE 2000) for practitioners working with children aged 3 to 6; and more recently the publication of *Birth to Three Matters, A Framework to Support Children in Their Earliest Years* (DfES 2002). Other chapters in this book provide a fuller background to the principles underlying the Framework, and the Aspects and Components covered in it. But from a policy perspective the publication of *Birth to Three Matters* (DfES 2002) marks a significant development in the recognition of the particular needs of our youngest children.

Every Child Matters

The Green Paper *Every Child Matters* (HM Treasury 2003) was hailed by the Prime Minister at its launch as the most important report in relation to children for the past 30 years. Published in response to the death of Victoria Climbié, whose plight was ignored by 12 different professionals, the Green Paper should lead to far-reaching changes in the way the needs of children are assessed, and the way in which services are planned and delivered. It has particular relevance to children from birth to 3, with its strong focus on better prevention, on earlier intervention, on better integration and on stronger support for parenting and families. It starts with five overall outcomes that should be our aim for all children:

- being healthy – enjoying good physical and mental health and living a healthy lifestyle;
- staying safe – being protected from harm and neglect;
- enjoying and achieving – getting the most out of life and developing the skills for adulthood;
- making a positive contribution – being involved with the community and society and not engaging in anti-social or offending behaviour;
- economic well-being – not being prevented by economic disadvantage from achieving their full potential.

Although these hardly feature in the main body of the report, it is to be hoped that they will inform the way in which quite different targets and sets of objectives are pulled together across both central and local government departments.

All five sections of the Green Paper have relevance to children under 3.

- Strong Foundations confirms support for Sure Start local programmes and the National Childcare Strategy, and for the National Service Framework for Children set up by the Department of Health which has a specific working group looking at improving maternity services and ante- and post-natal care. Both Sure Start local programmes and children's centres place a heavy emphasis on better links with health visitors and primary care teams.
- Supporting Parents and Carers promises improved support for parenting and families through universal and specialist services, including more involvement of parents in nurseries and schools, and a greater emphasis on home visiting programmes such as Home Start and on parent education programmes.
- Early Intervention and Effective Protection proposes improvements in information sharing across agencies, a common assessment framework, multidisciplinary teams of professionals to identify and work with children at risk, co-locating services in and around children's centres and schools, and ensuring effective child protection procedures are in place across all organizations.
- Accountability and integration at local, regional and national level includes the integration of several government departments under a new Minister for Children, Young People and Families. At the local level, there will be a requirement to establish joint machinery across education, health and social services for strategic planning and co-ordinated service delivery, as well as a new post of Director of Children's Services.
- Workforce Reform proposes the establishment of a Children's

Workforce Unit to develop a pay and workforce strategy for all who work with children, and the establishment of a sector skills council to deliver the strategy. This is likely to include work on a common core of training for all who work with children and families, and common occupational standards across all sectors.

Every Child Matters (HM Treasury 2003) presents an exciting and ambitious agenda, but it can only deliver if sufficient resources are found to add to the better use of existing resources that is envisaged.

Conclusion

The first seven years of a 'New Labour' Government have seen a huge number of policy developments in the early years, with an expansion of daycare and nursery education places, a growth in the number of children's centres providing more joined-up services for children and families, over 500 new Sure Start programmes, and a far greater recognition of the importance of the first three years of life. The over-arching focus on reducing the number of children living in poverty has led to a specific emphasis on increasing the amount of daycare available to enable parents to return to work, and although these developments have been welcomed, there are concerns about the quality of some nurseries, and concerns that some women are finding it hard to choose to stay at home to care for their children. There is pressure in some Sure Start schemes to move away from support for parents towards providing daycare places. Both daycare and family support are surely needed, particularly for those women who feel they have neither the confidence nor the skills to return straight away to the labour market. And there is a greater recognition of the key role that parents play in the lives of their small children, and of their need for support if they are to fulfil this role well.

The publication of the *Birth to Three Matters* Framework (DfES 2002) has been widely welcomed, and the subsequent training programme that followed should ensure that practitioners are able to take full advantage of what it has to offer.

The main policy challenges for the future are to extend the period of paid maternity/parental leave to enable those parents who might wish to do so to remain at home caring for their very young children; to continue the programme of expansion of accessible, high-quality and affordable provision; and to ensure that all those who care for children from birth to 3, whether in nurseries or in their own homes as childminders or relatives, do so with a greater understanding of the needs of very young children and how best to meet them.

References

Ball, M. (2002) *Getting Sure Start Started*, National evaluation of Sure Start, Report No. 2, July. London: Department for Education and Skills.

Blakemore, S. (2000) *Early Years Learning*, Post Report, June 2000, House of Commons Education and Employment Select Committee. London: House of Commons.

Bynner, J. (2001) Childhood risks and protective factors in social exclusion, *Children and Society*, 15: 285–301.

Day Care Trust (2003) *Towards Universal Childcare*. London: Day Care Trust.

Department of Health (2000) *The NHS Plan: A Plan for Investment, a Plan for Reform*. London: The Stationery Office.

DfES (2002) *Birth to Three Matters*. London: DfES Publications.

Glass, N. (1999) Sure Start: the development of an early intervention programme for young children in the UK, *Children and Society*, 13: 257–64.

HM Treasury (2003) *Every Child Matters* (the Green Paper). London: The Stationery Office.

Home Office (1998) *Supporting Families* (the Green Paper). London: The Stationery Office.

Oliver, C. and Smith, M. (2000) *Effectiveness of Early Interventions: Perspectives on Education Policy*. London: University of London, Institute of Education.

Pugh, G. (1998) *Children at Risk of Becoming Socially Excluded: An Introduction to 'The Problem'*, paper to HM Treasury seminar, January, Cross-departmental review of provision for young children.

Pugh, G. (2002) The consequences of inadequate investment in the early years, in J. Fisher (ed.) *The Foundations of Learning*. Buckingham: Open University Press.

Pugh, G. (2003) Children's centres and social inclusion, *Education Review*, 17: 23–9.

Pugh, G., De'Ath, E. and Smith, C. (1994) *Confident Parents, Confident Children: Policy and Practice in Parent Education and Support*. London: National Children's Bureau.

QCA/DfEE (2000) *Curriculum Guidance for the Foundation Stage*. London: QCA/DfEE.

Sammons, P., Sylva, K., Melhuish, E., Siraj-Blatchford, I., Taggart, B. and Elliot, K. (2002a) *Measuring the Impact of Preschool on Children's Cognitive Progress Over the Preschool Period*, Technical Paper 8a. London: Institute of Education.

Sammons, P., Sylva, K., Melhuish, E., Siraj-Blatchford, I., Taggart, B. and Elliot, K. (2002b) *Measuring the Impact of Preschool on Children's Social/Behavioural Development over the Preschool Period*, Technical Paper 8b. London: Institute of Education.

Sinclair, R., Hearn, B. and Pugh, G. (1997) *Preventive Work with Families: The Role of Main Stream Services*. London: National Children's Bureau.

4 Research Matters

Tricia David, Kathy Goouch and Sacha Powell

Introduction

To the authors of this chapter research matters very much. Each has been involved in a wide range of research projects both nationally and internationally. Individually they represent different specialisms and interests in the field of early childhood care and education. Collectively they contribute impressive research skills combined with a deep understanding of, and commitment to, young children and their families. Each has considerable practical experience of working with young children in a variety of early years settings. They succeed in making research accessible and demonstrate how it underpins all our work with young children. It is no wonder that they were the obvious team to write *Birth to Three Matters: A Review of the Literature* (David et al. 2003).

In this chapter we want to tell the 'story' of our 'adventure' in working on the review of research literature for the *Birth to Three Matters* Framework (DfES 2002). It was, at times, a hectic and arduous adventure, but always fascinating. Perhaps one of the most fascinating aspects of all was the fact that, like Peer Gynt, we found we had ended up where we started. What we were seeking was right there, 'at home'. We seemed to have confirmed our beliefs that babies come already 'designed', or 'programmed', to be deeply interested in people and the world in which they find themselves. Further, our view of them as incredibly observant and selective, as well as extremely clever at interpreting what they witness, was also confirmed. Added to that, the research reinforced our experiences – babies seem to learn best by playing with things they find in their world, and above all by playing with the familiar people who love them. So, the research we explored seemed to have supported our own views, derived from real-life experiences, that:

- more than anything else, young children need loving, responsive, sensitive key people around them; people who recognize their fascination with and curiosity about what is going on in their worlds, who will cater for their drive to explore and problem-solve through active learning, and who will provide opportunities to play, make friends and share experiences, and yet allow time for them to be deeply focused alone but near others, as well as ensuring all their health needs are met;

- they need to be respected as people in their own right; and
- they need to live in a society that is informed about their development and learning, and which is involved and delighted in their amazing abilities.

While this conclusion was in many ways comforting, it was also unsettling, because we had to ask ourselves whether the findings had come out this way because we were biased, blind to research that contradicted our own views. Or maybe it was because most of the research we had been able to access was based on the same assumptions and cultural expectations we ourselves hold. We are still asking those questions.

In the meantime, we will share with you the process we went through and more of the main conclusions we drew.

Why research matters

Research is important because it helps us make informed decisions. It may also challenge our thinking and actions, and be a form of protection against our own ignorance, or that of others whose actions might be harmful. Apart from anything else, in our own experience, research often provides exciting, thought-provoking insights.

Which research matters

As we had been asked to provide a background review of literature, mainly research literature, which concerned the development of children between birth and 3 years, the research we explored took this focus. It was a broad focus and encompassed research from many different disciplines. These included developmental psychology and medicine, as well as neurophysiology, linguistics and sociology. We could have included other disciplines, such as history, since much can be learnt from historical accounts about how babies and young children have been reared, but it was decided we should set boundaries as we wallowed in a cornucopia of evidence, so we set a limit of the last 20 years, except for work that we considered key texts from before that period (such as the works of Bowlby and Piaget).

In addition to this, we laid out criteria by which to judge the relevance of reported research and the appropriateness of the methods used, in order to make our review as rigorous as possible.

Although the majority of the review would be taken up with reporting on what we had found, it was thought necessary to include two introductory chapters in our document. One discusses the complex nature of children's development, for example raising issues related to the assumptions and values associated with certain research perspectives, or to particular views of early childhood. The other introductory chapter outlines some of the major theories that have influenced thinking about young children's development in Minority World countries, at the same time urging greater dissemination of theories from the Majority World. It also provides references to the research which led the proponent of a particular theory to reach their conclusions.

What we hoped to promote through these discussion chapters was, firstly, the sense that the people who spend their lives with babies and young children see the wonderful abilities of these competent little people every day. We felt that their important experiences should be reflected in the accounts of research. Secondly, we hoped to engender the idea that research is exciting and open to everyone. Thirdly, we needed to acknowledge that childhood is a cultural construction – that societies and children themselves co-construct what happens to and is expected of young children in a particular society. Fourthly, theories are meant to help us make sense of our worlds. We wanted to explain that we all develop theories, but if we are responsible for young children, especially those from other families to whom we are accountable, we need to be able to recognize and reflect on our theories, where they came from and how they influence our practice.

Systematic research reviews and how we conducted our review

At approximately the same time as we were engaging in the writing of *Birth to Three Matters: A Review of the Literature* (David et al. 2003), there was much debate in educational research circles about appropriate methodology for conducting rigorous reviews of research literature relevant to a particular topic. Naturally, we needed to take account of those debates. However, we were unable to restrict our review in the way the medical model being promoted required, because our topic had already been set for us. A second factor was the limited time available, which meant that it was not possible for more than one team member to read each piece of evidence. However, the overall project team, and Steering and Working Group members, were familiar with much of the material sourced. In fact, they and other colleagues, including many in other countries, recommended particular relevant texts to the review team.

Here is the process by which we carried out our searches and eliminated some of the references. Firstly, a list of key words and terms likely to generate published information about children's development during the years from birth to age 3 was developed. A second list of relevant databases and journals was also compiled. The team shared out the second list and, using the key terms, each searched allotted databases, for example the British Education Index (BEI), the Social Science Citation Index, OVID Biomed. A proforma was devised against which to check the relevance and rigour of a research report and its potential contribution to the review, while ensuring each team member adopted the same criteria for inclusion. Having scoured the titles and abstracts highlighted by these varied databases, each team member saved the results to computer disk, with the intention of using these in a second phase, to eliminate less relevant or overly repeated entries. The full texts of those titles and abstracts which then remained were followed up by the team members.

At first we had envisaged the review in a traditional way, with chapters detailing our findings about development under headings like 'cognitive development', 'affective development', and so on. However, we realized that it would be important to create the review using the *Birth to Three Matters* Framework (DfES 2002) with Aspects as chapter headings, so that the research information would be meaningful in relation to the Framework. We would also incorporate as many links as possible to the distilled child development information provided on the laminated cards. This information was being set out as sets of bullet points under the heading 'Development Matters', intended to act as sign-posts to young children's development and achievements in a particular area during their first three years of life. The inclusion of possible patterns of development was not intended to convey the idea that all children follow the same path but rather to indicate ways of understanding what children are trying to achieve, how they are attempting to gain some control over their own lives, and why the encouragement and support of adults and older children is important if they are to 'make sense' of the world in which they find themselves.

Initially, the task of writing a review with this structure seemed daunting – there would be so many links, so much inter-weaving! We suddenly recognized that the same would be true if the review were to be written with traditional headings, because young children's development is truly interwoven, or holistic. In reality this made the task more exciting, more of a challenge, to attempt to capture such real-life complexity.

While the review formed an integral part of the pack, being first published on the CD-ROM, it was also made available in book form and on the DfES website in 2003. As authors, we hoped the review would be helpful to practitioners working with babies and young children, and it was for this reason we decided we should write it in a slightly innovative way, with occasional anecdotes about real children, observed by members of the teams, to highlight the relevance and meaning of certain elements of the reported research findings.

So the review was organized according to the Aspects: A Strong Child, A Skilful Communicator, A Competent Learner and A Healthy Child – and within those chapters we tried to address each of the relevant Components and include 'stories' about children close to us.

What we found out about young children

It would not be possible here to detail all the research information from the whole review, so we have summarized the key 'messages' for each Aspect.

Key messages from research about A Strong Child

In the Framework *Birth to Three Matters* (DfES 2002), the Aspect entitled A Strong Child is concerned with the ways in which children's growing awareness of 'self' can be fostered in the years between birth and 3. During this phase, young children begin to show personal characteristics, preferences, capabilities and self-confidence. They play a part in contributing to attachments and explore emotional boundaries. It is now that they develop a sense of belonging.

The research literature provided information about how babies and young children are helped to be and to become competent and emotionally strong. Research over many years has shown that early experiences are very important in shaping children's emotional health, resilience and social competence, but this is not a *critical* (that is, once for all) situation – we should not assume that support and intervention in the earliest years guarantees later success, nor that early disadvantage cannot be overcome (Schaffer 1998; Rutter 1999; Clarke and Clarke 2000). A further important aspect to developing as A Strong Child emotionally and socially involves the child's sense of self and, according to research, this too depends on the sensitivity and responsiveness of that child's primary attachment figures – the small, significant group of adults and older children with whom they form their closest relationships. Babies and young children will seek to draw these people into interactions with them, by increased smiling, cooing, babbling and other attempts to promote intimacy, when they are nearby. They are helped to develop the confidence and self-assurance to become independent people with healthy self-esteem as a result of the strength they gain from these sensitive, responsive interactions. We found indications of how postnatal depression can mean it is difficult for a new mother to provide the kind of emotional support a new baby needs in order to develop these capacities rather than shutting down (see also Robinson 2003).

The research we explored also highlighted the ways in which children acquire the social practices related to particular emotions associated with the cultural group in which they are growing up, and how babies and young children develop a sense of belonging to a family and to other groups with which they are familiar (such as an education and care setting). For example, Judy Dunn (1993) found that children who enjoyed strong, positive attachments to their mothers were more likely, when a little older, to be conciliatory with friends and to enter elaborate, shared fantasy play bouts and conversations. Similarly, Howes et al. (1994) found that young children who felt secure with their educarer were more gregarious and engaged in complex play with other children. It was important to include evidence from research concerning attachment difficulties faced by some children with special needs (see, for example, Trevarthen et al. 1998).

Key messages from research about a Skilful Communicator

The research evidence accessed showed how early in life babies have the ability to distinguish the language spoken by their mother and other family members (heard *in utero*), from other languages (Karmiloff and Karmiloff-Smith 2001) and that they appear to enter the world with a drive to be near those familiar people, especially those with whom they develop 'primary intersubjectivity', which involves the rudiments of turn-taking, sensitive timing, responsiveness to others' behaviour and facial expressions. Early playful interactions of this type are called 'protoconversations' and they form the basis for the social and cognitive advances in the earliest years of life (for example, see Snow and Ferguson 1977; Murray and Andrews 2000; Trevarthen and Aitken 2001). Above all, the research showed that young children are brilliant observers who try to make sense of their worlds and to communicate effectively, often using a range of gestures and sometimes more than one language. Between 12 and 36 months of age they grasp what is and is not culturally acceptable behaviour and speech, and this is the result of being involved in interactions during the first year of life in which one is treated as if one is a person who understands and can respond. For example, 2½-year-old Oliver listened as his Mum asked his 4-year-old brother Kieran why he had been given a sticker by his reception teacher. When she congratulated Kieran, Oliver chimed in that he had one from nursery too. His Mum looked very pleased and asked why he had been awarded a sticker. 'For being good at buying cakes', he replied. He really had bought some cakes on a day when the nursery was fund-raising.

Key messages from research about A Competent Learner

The Aspect A Competent Learner focuses on the ability to make connections (for example, through the senses) and to begin to compare, categorize and classify. It also covers ideas about how babies and young children are imaginative and creative; and how, even at this stage, they can use symbols to represent thoughts and language. Babies only a few hours old gaze at patterns that resemble the human face in preference to random patterns, so we know that they can distinguish between people and the objects around them. So they seem to come into the world 'programmed' to prefer looking at human faces, human beings and movements, rather than simply at objects. Research evidence accumulated since the 1980s has meant that scientists have had to alter their assumptions and understandings about babies. Now, even newborns are thought to have an objective awareness of their surroundings (Bremner 1998). They search out patterns. This is how young children learn to discriminate and make connections between different objects and experiences. As connections are made, a child makes increasing sense of the world and does not have to wait until the onset of language to start thinking (Mandler 1999), but language and thought are developmentally linked and each promotes the development of the other. Trevarthen et al. (1998) report that research shows how the intimate, emotionally-laden paired interactions between a baby or young child and each of their significant others (loved, familiar adults or older children) form the foundations of cognitive development, the integration of personality and the ability to adapt socially.

Thirty years ago, Bruner (1972) argued that young animals play to learn and that the capacity for learning is related to the length of immaturity. During the first 3 years, babies and young children begin to rehearse roles, pretend and create play props, as their ability to imagine accelerates, along with their acquisition of language and their competent use of symbols in play (Bruce 2001). In the literature review, the processes (rather than products) of young children's activities are stressed, since, as Malaguzzi (1998), the founding thinker of the Reggio Emilia approach, suggested, young children construct and reinvent their ideas, they are not possessive about them, and so they continuously explore, share, make discoveries and transform their understandings, becoming attached to new and exciting forms and meanings that they experience. The *Review of the Literature* (David et al. 2003) includes evidence from research on mark-making and discusses young children's developing cognitive and creative abilities.

Key messages from research about A Healthy Child

The fourth Aspect of the Framework *Birth to Three Matters* (DfES 2002), A Healthy Child, brings together evidence about young children's mental and physical well-being. The research we reviewed includes not only issues related to physical health, such as having nutritious food and being free from illness (see, for example, BMA 1999), it provides a discussion of recent research about early brain development, as well as considering children's need to be special to someone. Health and social well-being underpin and determine children's responses to their environment, to people and to new experiences. Emotional well-being results from having close, warm and supportive relationships and being able to express feelings such as joy, grief, frustration and fear. Being supported and loved when one has these feelings leads to the development of coping strategies later in life, when faced with new, challenging or stressful situations. Meggitt (2001) suggests that there are six areas to be considered in relation to children's health: physical, mental, emotional, social, spiritual and environmental health, but basing her argument on her review of relevant research, she discusses health in holistic terms. In the review we provide information about genetic factors which can predispose young children to health problems, as well as factors related to poverty and conditions in the child's environment that can contribute to disadvantage.

While stressing the importance of positive early experiences and their impact on the rapid brain development during these first 3 years, the review explains that researchers in this field are cautious about claims that certain experiences or products can boost brainpower or make long-term differences. They do, however, talk of 'sensitive periods' when babies and young children may be especially receptive, and both neuroscientists and cognitive scientists suggest that playful interactions with parents and other significant people, in which there is talk, making funny faces and having fun together, affect brain development. Further, from around 18 months of age, interactions with other children provide the stimuli for 'redesigning' one's brain, as one comes to realize that others have minds too and that these are different from our own (see, for example, Bruer 1997; Gopnik et al. 1999; Johnson 2002). Siegel's (1999) research on brain development and memory indicates the important role of shared narratives, or stories, about our own and others' lives, in the ability to organize the mind, create coherent internal integration and to make sense of other minds.

The review also includes evidence from research issues concerning safety and abuse, as well as that considering difficult behaviour and what it may mean. Research and evaluation reports on early intervention programmes in both the USA and the UK include the following points, indicating the need to:

- move to a 'joined-up' model of delivery;
- build on the model of Sure Start in areas of moderate disadvantage;
- build the potential of parents and para-professionals for effective and cost-effective identification and intervention;
- harness the natural involvement of parents to build parenting skills;
- provide for accreditation of prior experience and learning towards qualifications for para-professionals;
- provide training for early childhood education and care personnel which bridges the health–education divide;
- provide training through a variety of models, including distance and part-time residential courses;
- improve inter-agency communication, understanding and mutual respect;
- ring-fence funding for identification and intervention for children from 0 to 2;
- fund further research;
- disseminate effective practice;
- respect children's and parents' rights.
  (adapted from Fawcett 2001: 11–12)

Ramey and Ramey reviewed a number of such reports and collated the conclusions into six principles about the potential efficacy of intervention programmes. They suggest attention should be paid to:

- developmental timing (the younger the child is enrolled and the longer the intervention, the greater the benefits, although there is no evidence of critical periods);
- programme intensity (greater intensity, for example, by number of home visits per week, produces greater effects);
- direct intervention (intervention professionals and para-professionals need to work with the children themselves as well as with parents, although Ramey and Ramey stress the importance of celebrating parents' and other family members' contributions as primary carers);
- programme breadth and flexibility (comprehensive and multi-route programmes generally have larger effects);
- individuals, because individuality matters (that is, match the intervention to the child's or family's need);
- the intervention needs to be ecologically pervasive and maintained (early years interventions alone may not be enough, whole communities, involving local schools, for example, tend to be more effective).
  (adapted from Ramey and Ramey 1998: 115–17)

Many of the government's recent initiatives, such as Sure Start, the National Parenting Institute, and the expanded role of health visitors are therefore encouraging developments because they are intended to comply with the principles set out in both Fawcett's (2001) and Ramey and Ramey's (1998) conclusions.

The key research messages

A final summary of the conclusions we reached as a result of carrying out the review yielded the following.

- All areas of learning and development are intricately intertwined, young children develop and learn holistically and their emotional and social development seems to form the bedrock of other developmental areas.
- Babies seem to come into the world primed for attachment to warm familiar carers, who will usually be mothers, fathers, grandparents, older brothers and sisters and key adults in early childhood education and care settings.
- These attachments form the basis for subsequent relationships, and for a person's sense of self and self-assurance. Those children who have had experience of warm attachments and positive responses become socially adept, self-assured, independent and interdependent, higher achievers in their later early childhood education and care and school settings.
- Parents who express negative narratives concerning their own early relationships with their parents need support to overcome perpetuating such patterns and to form joyful, mutually loving relationships with their babies and small children.
- Babies are born with the ability to perceive differences in languages and they can recognize the sounds used in the languages spoken in their homes.
- Between 12 and 36 months of age, young children grasp what is and is not culturally acceptable behaviour and speech, and this is the result of being involved in interactions during the first year of life, in which one is treated as if one is a person who understands and can respond.
- Babies seem to be tuned to learn from, with and about, firstly the people and the cultural environment around them, followed by the material environment – they come into the world primed to be curious, competent learners.

- Play, in which the baby or child takes the lead and makes choices, is a process which fosters cognitive development.
- Language and thought are developmentally linked; they each depend on and also promote the development of the other.
- Children 'make sense' of and 'transform' knowledge, experiences and events through imaginative and creative activity.
- Children's developing memories and use of narrative help them make sense of their lives.
- They want to share and express their ideas playfully through the 'hundred languages of children' (for example, dancing, singing, talking, 'storying', music-making, painting, making patterns, building, model-making, 'animating' puppets and other toys, dressing up, gardening, looking after animals, drawing, mark-making, to list but a few possibilities).
- Once again, the research points to the centrality of positive relationships with parents and other key people in young children's lives.

What we found out about early childhood education and care research

The review process identified gaps in the research available, despite the wide range of disciplines covered by the search. For example, there is a paucity of evidence about processes and practices in early childhood education and care for children from birth to 3 years. In particular, the field needs research information about toddlers in early childhood education and care settings, as well as exploring the impact of practitioner training on the experiences of children and parents.

By linking this review with another we were involved in for the British Educational Research Association Early Years Special Interest Group (BERA Early Years SIG 2003), we found further 'gaps' in research about young children, such as the relative lack of research into young children's learning in the arts, humanities, physical education or spiritual and moral education in early childhood education and care settings; and that more research is needed on the outcomes for children of different types of staff training.

Another area in which research evidence is limited is that linking early childhood education and care and parental employment, particularly from the child's point of view, despite this being a key area mentioned by parents when they explain their difficulties in juggling employment with the upbringing of very young children.

As far as the review, *Birth to Three Matters: A Review of the Literature* (David et al. 2003), is concerned, there were many other areas we could have included, given more time – and space! For example, a review of the large body of literature concerning parents might have provided very useful knowledge for the field.

Concluding messages

From the review of the research, we concluded that practitioners need to be able to:

- understand attachment and the importance of a child being special to at least one significant person in order to promote resilience;
- be informed about young children's development;
- provide opportunities to explore and play in a safe and secure environment – children's mobility and movement are important for their development;
- know about brain development and the importance of 'nourishment' (a good diet, in the form of both food and of physical and psychological stimulation);
- help parents see that intimate behaviours such as 'bugging' and nudging, pet names and idiosyncratic behaviour are important and that children's development sometimes seems difficult because they are trying to become independent people with a sense of self;
- have reasonable rules which fit with children's rhythms and give a pattern to life;
- know that parents, as well as children, need support;
- know about child abuse and neglect and have other colleagues to consult;
- recognize the additional requirements of babies and young children with special needs, and plan how to ensure these children have access to similar experiences and opportunities to their peers;
- help communities and the public understand the importance of positive interactions and experiences in the first three years for all areas of development, including brain development, and for enjoyment in the here and now;
- access the education and training necessary in order to fulfil their important role.

Above all, while the review process did not throw up any surprises for the review team, the wealth of research evidence which exists in this multi-professional, multidisciplinary field astounded us. Further, since most of this evidence has not been made available before to the field of early childhood education and care in a review of this kind, we felt very privileged to have been involved in its production.

In the review, our concluding chapter provides three tightly focused pointers, setting out the main implications we derived from our 'adventure' for each of the following groups: children, parents, practitioners, policy makers, trainers and researchers. The unsurprising conclusions we reached concerning babies and young children are that:

- they need loving, responsive, sensitive key people around them, people who recognize their fascination with and curiosity about what is going on in their world, who cater for their drive to explore and problem solve through active learning, and who will provide opportunities to play, make friends and share experiences, and yet allow time for them to be deeply focused alone but near others, as well as ensuring all their health needs are met;
- they should be respected as people in their own right; and
- they should live in a society which is informed about their development and learning, and which is involved and delighted in their amazing abilities.

The question that remains for debate, however, is how, as a society and as a field, we set about ensuring the fulfilment of these apparently obvious and simple conclusions.

References

BERA Early Years SIG (2003) *Early Years Research: Pedagogy, Curriculum and Adult Roles, Training and Professionalism*. Southwell, Notts: BERA.

BMA (1999) *Growing up in Britain: Ensuring a Healthy Future for our Children – A Study of 0–5 Year Olds*. London: British Medical Association.

Bremner, G. (1998) From perception to action: the early development of knowledge, in F. Simion and G. Butterworth (eds) *The Development of Sensory, Motor and Cognitive Capacities in Early Infancy. From Perception to Cognition*. Hove: Psychology Press: 239–56.

Bruce, T. (2001) *Learning through Play: Babies, Toddlers and the Foundation Years*. London: Hodder and Stoughton.

Bruer, J. (1997) Education and the brain: a bridge too far? *Educational Researcher*, 26(8): 4–16.

Bruner, J.S. (1972) The nature and uses of immaturity, *American Psychologist*, 27: 1–23.

Clarke, A. and Clarke, A. (2000) *Early Experience and the Life Path*. London: Jessica Kingsley Open Books.

David, T., Goouch, K., Powell, S. and Abbott, L. (2003) *Birth to Three Matters: A Review of the Literature. (Research Report 444)*. Nottingham: DfES Publications.

DfES (2002) *Birth to Three Matters*. London: DfES Publications.

Dunn, J. (1993) *Young Children's Close Relationships. Beyond Attachment*. Newbury Park, California: Sage.

Fawcett, A. (2001) *Special Educational Needs/Early Years Literature Review. A Report to the Department for Education and Skills*. Sheffield: University of Sheffield.

Gopnik, A., Melzoff, A. and Kuhl, P. (1999) *How Babies Think: The Science of Childhood*. London: Weidenfeld and Nicolson.

Howes, C., Hamilton, C.E. and Matheson, C.C. (1994) Children's relationships with peers: differential associations with aspects of the teacher-child relationship, *Child Development*, 65 (1): 253–63.

Johnson, M. (2002) Brain building, *Interplay*, Summer: 36–42.

Karmiloff, K. and Karmiloff-Smith, A. (2001) *Pathways to Language: From Fetus to Adolescent*. Cambridge, Mass.: Harvard University Press.

Malaguzzi, L. (1998) History, ideas, and basic philosophy, in C. Edwards, L. Gandini and G. Foreman (eds) *The Hundred Languages of Children*. New York: Ablex.

Mandler, J. (1999) Preverbal representation and language, in P. Bloom, M. Peterson, L. Nadel and M. Garrett (eds) *Language and Space*. Cambridge, Mass.: A Bradford Book/MIT Press: 365–84.

Meggitt, C. (2001) *Baby and Child Health*. Oxford: Heinemann Educational Publishers.

Murray, L. and Andrews, E. (2000) *Social Baby*. London: Richmond Press.

Ramey, C.T. and Ramey, S.L. (1998) Early intervention and early experience, *American Psychologist*, 53(2): 109–20.

Robinson, M. (2003) *From Birth to One: The Year of Opportunity*. Buckingham: Open University Press.

Rutter, M. (1999) Psychosocial adversity and child psychopathology, *British Journal of Psychiatry*, 174: 480–93.

Schaffer, H.R. (1998) *Making Decisions about Children: Psychological Questions and Answers*. Oxford: Blackwell.

Siegel, D. (1999) *The Developing Mind*. New York: Guilford.

Snow, C.E. and Ferguson, C.A. (eds) (1977) *Talking to Children*. Cambridge: Cambridge University Press.

Trevarthen, C. and Aitken, K. (2001) Infant intersubjectivity: research, theory, and clinical applications, *Journal of Child Psychology and Psychiatry*, 42(1).

Trevarthen, C., Aitken, K., Papoudi, D. and Robarts, J. (1998) *Children with Autism: Diagnosis and Interventions to Meet their Needs*. London: Jessica Kingsley.

5 Practitioners Matter

Helen Moylett and Pat Djemli

Introduction

Helen Moylett and Pat Djemli have been closely involved with *Birth to Three Matters* (DfES 2002) since its conception: Helen, as a member of the Steering and Working Groups, and long-suffering head of one of the centres regularly invaded by video cameras and requests to trial materials; Pat, as Care Manager, was responsible for the under 3s and family support, and as the Advanced Skills Practitioner (ASP) on a subsequent project has supported practitioners in her own Centre and in a range of settings within the community. To both of them, practitioners matter a great deal, and in the new posts to which they have recently been appointed, Helen as one of the Regional Directors for the Foundation Stage, and Pat as a Training Officer, they are continuing to support practitioners.

In this chapter they share their practice and their views on why practitioners are so important in working with children from birth to 3 and their families.

We believe that the quality of the staff team is the most important factor in ensuring good-quality education and care for children and support for parents and carers. One of the principles underpinning *Birth to Three Matters* (DfES 2002) is 'Caring adults count more than resources and equipment'. There are 30 caring adults employed at Tamworth Early Years Centre in a variety of roles. In this chapter we use examples from everyday life at the centre to explore some of the ways in which these practitioners matter to children, to families, to each other and to society generally. Clearly we will be focusing on staff who work with the very youngest children, but the rest of the team also contribute to the centre ethos and the ways in which policies on crucial areas such as inclusion and learning and teaching are translated into practice. This chapter is in many ways a tribute to all our colleagues – support staff, teachers and nursery nurses.

The following brief pen portrait of the centre provides a context for the next four sections. Tamworth Early Years Centre opened in 2001. It brought together two existing nurseries (a maintained nursery school and a social services day nursery) and two staff teams, as well as other professionals, in the refurbished nursery school building. The centre is jointly funded by education and social services and provides high-quality integrated education and care for children aged 1 to 5. We have up to 20 places and two rooms for the youngest children: 'Teddies' for children who are aged 1 to 2 and 'Tigers' for the 2- to 3-year-olds. These two rooms are connected by a bathroom and shared messy area and children move between them and also into the outdoor area and the much larger over 3s nursery when appropriate. All the children in Teddies and Tigers are referred by social services and/or health. The centre staff who work with them are all also involved in a range of support programmes and initiatives to help families and other carers. All of them are qualified to at least NVQ 3 level.

In order to make the most of the abilities with which they are born, young children need competent, consistent adults to care for them and support their learning and development. The practitioners who work with very young children need not only to be well qualified and knowledgeable but also extremely sensitive to the holistic nature of children's learning. Working with a curriculum which flows from the child, which enmeshes care and education and which cannot be neatly divided into subjects or areas of learning can be very demanding.

Practitioners matter to children

> In order for professionals to work effectively with babies, young children and their parents, their first duty is to recognize themselves for who they are, what they believe and why. The emotions we see in infants and young children do not only belong to them, they belong to us. We have all been helpless infants, we all carry with us our history including that of being parented and therefore, consciously or unconsciously, we know what children are going through.
>
> (Robinson 2003: 171)

Robinson argues that, although we may know at some level what they are experiencing, many factors may conspire to make it difficult for us to empathize with children. Most of these are linked to our own emotional state and the ethos of the setting in which we work. Of course there is no such thing as the perfect practitioner or the perfect place to work. As Gopnik et al. (1999) observe when exploring how children come to understand the mind, 'completely understanding ourselves and other people is an arduous, lifelong business', but we know that children need positive interactions with adults and that confident adults make for confident children. Practitioners who are tuned in to children and to themselves as autonomous individuals are more likely to be effective and confident. Confident practitioners are not looking over their shoulders for managers, parents, Office for Standards in Education (OFSTED) or anyone else; they are looking straight at the children.

The following example of an everyday interaction at snack time is, we feel, a good example of two confident practitioners' commitment to a child and his learning.

Tom is 18 months old and attends the centre on two days per week. He has only just learned to walk and says a few single words. His face often appears expressionless but he likes to watch activities and after several months has begun to join in more willingly with messy and exploratory play. However, he usually waits for staff to make choices for him, for example with food and drink. Recently his key worker was very excited because he had made a choice for himself and got what he wanted.

Sitting at the table for snack with four other children and two adults, Tom did not indicate whether he wanted banana or pear when asked, so one of the practitioners cut a small piece off a banana and offered it to him. He pointedly ignored the piece she was offering and, keeping an eye on her, reached out his hand and took the rest of the banana from the plate on the table and put it straight in his mouth. His action was rewarded by smiles and approbation from his key worker and the other practitioner present, and Tom kept the banana he had chosen.

This action was regarded as a milestone for Tom and recorded as such in his profile. He is gradually becoming more communicative and more confident, although he still needs the frequent reassurance of his key worker and other familiar adults. The reactions of the practitioners in this scenario seem to be based on the following beliefs:

- a first step towards getting one's own needs met is to be clear about what one wants;
- children are not always predictable – the adult may present one or two choices and the child may find a third possibility;
- if this is safe for themselves and others, adults should go with it;
- all children are different and need to have their particular needs supported;
- children know when adults really value them;
- we should focus on what children can do rather than what they cannot do; and
- undervaluing children leads to them underperforming.

To unpack these principles a bit further, let's look at what might have happened if Tom's action had not been greeted positively and the practitioners had been working with a different set of beliefs.

The practitioners might have frowned at him, laughed at (rather than with) him, he might have had the banana taken from his hand, he might have been told he was 'naughty', he might have been told that there was only one banana and it had to be shared with the other children. All these reactions might seem reasonable to people who prioritize the following beliefs:

- when given a choice, the child should choose from the practitioner's menu not his own;
- young children are wilful and selfish and need to learn as early as possible to share;
- good manners are very important and need to be encouraged; and
- other children will copy bad manners.

Of course these two sets of beliefs are not necessarily mutually exclusive. One can, for example, think that generally good manners are very important, but not prioritize them with a child like Tom who needs much encouragement just to express his own needs and wants. One can feel that sharing is a very important life skill but recognize that it is often very difficult (even for adults) and that, until one begins to develop a theory of mind, it is almost impossible. A child who still finds it difficult to express his own wants will find it even more difficult to understand the wants of others.

This short anecdote illustrates how important the everyday interactions between staff and children are. Tom made a choice, it was valued and he is gradually gaining in confidence and assertiveness – becoming A Strong Child. If his choice had not been valued it seems very unlikely that he would subsequently have felt confident to make other choices and express other needs. The child of Tom's age who always sits quietly and passively waits for others to come to her/him is a child who should normally be a cause for concern rather than celebration, yet we have been in settings where quietness and passivity are encouraged.

Obviously Tom is helped to make choices throughout the day, not just at snack time. The banana incident is just one example of the sort of mundane interaction that goes on with very young children in every setting every day. However, it is this sort of incidental learning that matters just as much as the often over-planned 'focus' or 'adult-led' activity. If we believe that care and education are inseparable, what evidence do we have of that belief in action?

Practitioners matter to families

Along with care and education being inseparable, another well-loved and often declared belief is that parents are their children's first educators and we therefore need to work in partnership with them. And of course working with babies and very young children inevitably means having regular contact with their parents and carers.

Whatever their circumstances, parents and carers will need to build up a high level of trust in the practitioners with whom they leave their child. The National Childcare Strategy is aimed at encouraging parents back to work. Whatever sort of provision a parent chooses, starting or returning to work can be an extremely traumatic time and the parent will need to feel total confidence in the person who will be caring for their child. Equally those parents and carers who are not working will also feel separation anxiety, and children will come to any setting with differing levels of confidence and experiences of separation from their main carer.

All staff at Tamworth Early Years Centre are aware of the importance of offering parents and children a warm welcome and having an open and friendly manner. We know that feeling valued right from the start is the key to good relationships with parents and carers. One way we establish informality and equality is that we are all known by our first names. However, this was a big discussion point before the staff teams joined forces.

There is not space here to explore all the reasons for practitioners' views in this area. But perhaps some of the questions we asked ourselves are illuminating:

- What makes us 'professional' in our own and others' eyes?
- What messages do we give to students, support staff, children, parents and other visitors if we call them by their first names and insist on having a title ourselves?
- Are professionals working in social services, the youth and community service, less professional or more in tune with their client groups than education staff sometimes are?

Traditions and feeling comfortable with the decision needs to be taken into account, but at Tamworth we have found that this certainly makes the staff appear approachable and gives a feeling of equality amongst the staff team as a whole.

Like most early years settings we run courses, workshops and family learning sessions for parents. These are usually informal and hands on and we always ask parents what they want. Most parents are keen to help their children in any way they can and they appreciate opportunities to try out activities both as an adult group and with their children. It is important that they understand our philosophy and practice and that we de-mystify *Birth to Three Matters* (DfES 2002) and the *Curriculum Guidance for the Foundation Stage* (QCA/DfEE 2000), but it is also important that we do not patronize them or treat them as if they are at school. Parents and carers also join in cross-centre initiatives like emotional well-being for adults and children. We also provide support for families in a range of other ways. One major part of our family support work is Family Day.

Family Day happens once a week and was created to offer the children who attend the centre time to spend together with family members and staff who know them. It is an opportunity for practitioners and parents to share information, concerns, successes and progress. Each child arrives with their own life experiences and backgrounds. There is plenty of research that indicates that these need to be known and valued and the parent or carer will have vital information that needs to be shared with the practitioner who is caring for their child. Significant adults in the child's life need to be consulted, as well as birth parents. This includes significant males, and 'men only' days are always well attended and appreciated. We only have one male member of staff and it is easy to underestimate how difficult it can be for men to feel comfortable in what is traditionally seen as a female context.

As well as listening to parents, staff can share expertise informally on Family Day. Different stages of development can cause stress and tensions. Practitioners can offer advice and assistance to ease parents and children through these often emotive times, such as meal times or toilet training. Knowing that what your child is demonstrating is a 'normal' part of a young child's development can be reassurance in itself. If it is cause for further concern the practitioner can offer advice and strategies for coping.

Some parents have had difficult upbringings and want to offer their children something different. But the problem is the only role model they have had is one that they do not want. Parents look to practitioners to help them instigate change. Implementing change is not about imposing our values and beliefs on other people but more about helping them explore alternatives. Practitioners are able to offer a choice of alternative, more positive role models.

Examples have often centred on alternatives for behaviour management. Parents often do not want to smack their child as they know from experience this does not work. They want their child to feel loved and cherished but find it difficult when they may rarely have received any positive feedback themselves. Positive parenting can be explained by practitioners, as well as role-modelled, and help given to implement the strategies. Practitioners acknowledge what a difficult job parenting is, how easy it is to decline into that spiralling helter-skelter of criticism, and that most people need help to reverse the cycle. Every small step needs encouragement and praise for the parent as well as the child.

As we mentioned before, we offer many different sessions to parents and carers. Family Day is an opportunity for parents to practise skills and strategies introduced in those sessions with the practitioners present to offer support. For instance, many parents who have not had the joys and pleasures of exploring and discovering play themselves can hardly be expected to engage their children in meaningful play. Practitioners can not only extol the benefits of play for their children's development, but offer opportunities for parents to participate in the sheer enjoyment and bonding that is created. The calming and relaxing sensation of water play and gloop; the exhilarating feeling of splash painting; the defusing effect of clay bashing; the fun and laughter of dressing up; the closeness when sharing a book – the list is endless. Opportunities are created for parents and children to share these special times and can have a marked effect on the parent–child relationship.

Family Day is really important for developing trust and confidence in each other. However, this trust and confidence can be tested when child protection issues are identified. It is imperative that the child protection procedures are transparent to all parents and staff in order for actions to be clear. However sound the relationship between the practitioner and the parent, our experience is that the parent will still feel let down if the child protection procedures are instigated. They may also be embarrassed and feel they are being judged as 'bad' parents. It may be easy for the practitioner to collude with the parent or excuse their actions. However, the child's welfare is of paramount importance and concerns about a child need to be shared with relevant professionals. Clarity and openness about procedures may be the starting point for rebuilding a relationship.

However, the other side of the coin is that parents who feel they need help are at times able to confide in a practitioner rather than contacting the Social Services Department direct, and then are happy for the practitioner to make the referral on their behalf. The fact that parents are welcomed to the centre, where staff members are actively listening, encourages people to identify problems or concerns at a much earlier stage and this preventative approach can prevent situations arriving at crisis point. Attempting to teach people to swim during a storm in the middle of an ocean is a tactic we try to avoid.

Clearly supporting families as well as educating and caring for their children can be a difficult and stressful job and staff need to support each other.

Practitioners matter to each other

Those who have worked in settings where they have felt unsupported by their colleagues will know what a lonely place that can be. If we do not feel valued by those with whom we work, it is very difficult to decentre from our own concerns and value children and their families. As Elfer (2003) points out, the intense emotional demands of working with babies and toddlers 'remains one of the most neglected areas in early years practice'.

Having set up a centre which brought two main groups of staff together from education and social services backgrounds with several new staff and a brief to work with other agencies, we knew we had to talk to each other continually in order to share ideas and concerns and to begin to develop a common vision for where the centre was going. In the last two years the following initiatives have helped us recognize how much we all matter to each other. They have also helped to develop an ethos in which we have high expectations of ourselves and others alongside a recognition that we are all human and that openness and honesty about mistakes and concerns make us all stronger and more able to support each other.

- weekly team meetings (for over 3s and under 3s teams);
- fortnightly meetings for all over 3 and under 3 staff (with re-presentation from support staff);
- regular supervision;
- professional development opportunities for all staff.

We know it is not always easy to prioritize staff development and in some settings it will be easier than others. We have had to look very carefully at working patterns, funding and time management, but we believe that time for reflection and opportunities for professional dialogue are vital if we are going to build a confident team of practitioners who can offer the best service to children and their families.

Our weekly and fortnightly team meetings are vital for sharing information, policy making, raising concerns and planning events. Although these are all 'formal' meetings in the sense that they are timetabled, have an agenda and are minuted, they are informal in tone and anyone can put items on the agenda. They ensure that all members of staff have access to decision-making and know that their individual voices can be heard by everyone. Staff also meet in smaller groups for areas such as planning, working parties, interest groups, special needs support. However, it is also important that they have opportunities for individual support as well.

All staff meet their line manager for regular supervision/performance management/professional development review sessions (terminology depends on the tradition within which one works). We tend to call this process supervision but the importance is in the process rather than the name. It involves agreeing an agenda based on individual professional development needs, the centre development plan (including local and national priorities) and the needs of the children for whom individual staff members are responsible. It is led by the practitioner and is uninterrupted and confidential time. This is an important way of introducing practitioners to the importance of self-review and a reflective approach to their own work and that of the centre.

At these sessions professional development opportunities are discussed and reviewed. All staff attend the equivalent of five whole centre training days as well as other appropriate training and courses. However, continuing professional development is more than course attendance and involvement in projects. We are involved in *Birth to Three Training Matters*, which involves researching one's own practice, linking with other early years centres across the country, and working together with a group of providers from the private and voluntary sector. This is a really effective way of getting staff to reflect upon and improve their own practice, which in turn leads to more confidence. We encourage all staff to be involved in the centre's dissemination of effective practice by working with visitors and leading and contributing to workshops and talks.

At the time of writing we are working towards our Inclusion Quality Mark. Inclusion means more than complying with statutes or codes of practice. It means making positive statements about everybody's worth in what we do and say. Confident staff who feel welcome and valued in their place of work and who can articulate the theory and practice of the learning and teaching in which they are engaged, will find it much easier to welcome and value children, parents and visitors.

Practitioners matter to society

That practitioners matter to society may seem obvious as we are working with society's future – its children – at a time when their brains are at their most receptive and when they will learn more than they ever will again. However, working with young children has traditionally been seen as women's work, having low status and low pay.

Most practitioners will have been on the receiving end of the two stock responses to information about their role – what we call the 'teddy bear' or the 'monster'. Either 'Aaaah. How lovely being able to play all day, they're so sweet at that age!' or 'Oh no. How do you put up with all that noise all day?!' These may be stereotypes, but they often mask a contempt for our work, or at least ignorance and outdated ideas about children and childhood.

In 2002, Pugh, writing about the huge explosion in funding and initiatives we have seen in the early years, said 'the Cinderella of education, early years, is now on her way to the ball'. She was right, we have never had it so good, but as she also pointed out, 'While nursery teachers share the terms and conditions of their colleagues, other early years workers endure low pay and poor conditions of service, and many are still inadequately trained'.

Of course, if we were really in a fairy story like Cinderella we could wave a magic wand and make sure we all lived happily ever after in a world where early years workers were all trained to at least NVQ Level 3 and central government was working towards an all-graduate profession. However, the reality

is that training enough workers (50 per cent according to present requirements) to NVQ Level 2 is seen as a huge challenge in order to set up and
sustain sufficient childcare places.

As Moss pointed out:

> ... early childhood services and young children have become items
> on the agenda of two major and related [government] projects ...
> improving educational standards in school and increasing labour
> market participation and economic competitiveness. Viewed from
> the perspective of these imperative projects, young children are un-
> derstood primarily as dependents of their parents, in need of
> 'childcare', to enable their parents' employment and as 'becoming'
> school children and economically active adults.
>
> (1999: 235)

The role of work in combating social exclusion should not be underestimated. Then why does it seem that people who are unable to articulate
clear ideas for future employment, or who are starting from a very low qualification base, are often referred to the caring professions, usually childcare or
to working with the elderly? We are lucky to work in a centre where we are all
qualified to at least NVQ Level 3. We know that many practitioners are doing
a good job with NVQ Level 2 or lower-level qualifications, but how can we
raise the status of the job when it is seen as just that – a job rather than a
career?

Those of us who work with the youngest children have to be ambassadors
at the highest levels for early childhood as a stage in its own right, for young
children as human beings rather than human becomings. However, it is very
difficult to take on this role if one is underpaid and undervalued by society.
For a profession that puts high importance on developing self-esteem in
others we undermine ourselves by not actively promoting ourselves as professionals. Society will only appreciate how much practitioners matter when
we start realizing it ourselves.

There is a wide diversity of ways in which childcare and education is
offered. But there is almost an underlying 'tier' system operating. Workers
employed by the mainstream sector enjoy much more appealing terms and
conditions and better rates of pay than those in the private and voluntary
sectors. Recruitment and retention is a problem when the pay is low, especially among male carers. On the other hand, there are many people sincerely
interested in and capable of pursuing a career in childcare yet one of the
biggest barriers to them achieving this appears to be lack of funding for
training. Whilst the status of the early years services is being elevated, the
status for the professional in early years still has a long way to go.

We have written earlier in this chapter about why we all matter in various ways and we would like to conclude by referring again to the *Birth to Three Training Matters* project. This has delivered funding to bring a wide range of practitioners in Tamworth together with a common purpose – to offer the best for the youngest children and their families by using the *Birth to Three Matters* Framework (DfES 2002). The Framework acknowledges the diversity of early years workers yet values them all and unites their qualities. It can be used in all settings.

Part of the project programme was to name two practitioners in each of five centres around the country to be Researchers and Advanced Skills Practitioners (ASPs). The ASPs work in and from the centres involved and act as mentors to a geographical cluster of childcare workers. In Tamworth this support was offered in the formation of a Cluster Group for all childcare providers in the area. Exploring the implications for implementing the *Birth to Three Matters* Framework (DfES 2002) was the purpose of taking this approach. The meetings held have actually highlighted the similarities of issues being experienced by everyone. We were also able to mind map the different types of solutions that were needed for the range of settings present. The group members have offered a wealth of experience and are able to give each other support and advice. For example, someone working in a day nursery setting was able to offer support to a childminder on how to adapt a particular plan for use in the home; expectations and fears about OFSTED were explored along with parental expectations. Different ways of implementing heuristic play have been investigated. Practitioners have tried things out and reported back to each other – they have all become active researchers of their own practice. Underpinning all the activities has been a commitment to sharing and exploring together. We are sure that all the practitioners involved in the project have gained in confidence and knowledge about young children and each other. This is a good model for professional development and could feed into further qualifications, it is relatively cheap and is based on reflective practice.

It is similar to many initiatives such as Best Practice Research, the Leadership Programme and many other projects which are centrally funded and open to teachers and other colleagues in schools. Perhaps we need to look more closely at such projects as well as trying to get 50 per cent of workers trained.

We are of course told that we cannot afford to pay more to nursery nurses, crèche workers, support assistants, childminders, playgroup workers, portage staff and all the others who educate and care for our most precious resource. Unfortunately their status is linked to the status we afford mothering. Greer (1999) argues for a rethinking of this status and the concomitant payment of mothers and teachers in a more just society. We would extend her argument to include other workers with young children.

In our own rich societies poor children present serious social problems; the modish term for it is 'social exclusion'. The socially excluded are people with no stake in society. It ought to be obvious
that people will only invest in society if society has invested in them.
In a rich society every child born is entitled to a decent living. The
primary carer who socializes and nurtures her/him is entitled to our
support, gratitude and respect. The teachers who continue the process are entitled to prestige and significant reward. We will be told
that we cannot afford to pay mothers and teachers, but of course we
can. All we have to do is shift priorities.

(Greer 1999: 322)

Since 1997 we have begun a process of shifting priorities and we have
made significant shifts – the *Birth to Three Matters* Framework (DfES 2002) is
one example – let's keep shifting, secure in the knowledge that nothing
matters more.

References

DfES (2002) *Birth to Three Matters*. London: DfES Publications.

Elfer, P. (2003) Close encounters, *Nursery World*, 30 January.

Gopnik, A., Meltzoff, A. and Kuhl, P. (1999) *How Babies Think*. London: Weidenfeld and Nicholson.

Greer, G. (1999) *the whole woman*. London: Doubleday.

Moss, P. (1999) Renewed hopes and lost opportunities: early childhood in the
early years of the Labour government, *Cambridge Journal of Education*, 29 (2):
229–38.

Pugh, G. (2002) Starting Right, *Times Education Supplement*, 21 June.

QCA/DfEE (2000) *Curriculum Guidance for the Foundation Stage*. London: QCA/
DfEE.

Robinson, M. (2003) *From Birth to One: The Year of Opportunity*. Buckingham: Open
University Press.

6 Quality Matters

Ann Langston and Lesley Abbott

Introduction

In writing this chapter we have focused on issues that seemed relevant to our work in the development of *Birth to Three Matters* (DfES 2002). The pursuit of quality is what has guided us in this endeavour and in this chapter we discuss some of the factors that have concerned us, which we call 'reasonable doubts', as well as those which we hope will ensure that babies, young children and their parents will always encounter quality in out of home settings.

That quality matters for young children and their families in daycare is indisputable. However, the way one begins to quantify or measure quality is fraught with difficulties since perceptions of quality vary with time, location, experience, history and so forth. Indeed, Moss and Pence have argued for a relativist approach, suggesting 'Quality in early childhood services is a constructed concept, subjective in nature and based on values, beliefs and interest, rather than an objective and universal reality. Quality childcare is, to a large extent, in the eye of the beholder' (1994: 5). It is not surprising, therefore, that definitions of quality have increasingly focused on measurable items such as the space and furnishings, activities and the curriculum, parent partnership, policy and management, and so on, described by Siraj-Blatchford and Wong as 'an objectivist approach' encompassing 'a collection of measurable characteristics in the childcare environment that affects children's social and cognitive development' (1999: 10). The purpose of this chapter is to consider how these dichotomous positions can be reconciled.

Birth to Three Matters (DfES 2002) is described as 'a framework to support children in their earliest years', yet its other expressed intention is to support 'effective practice' with the age group. Effective practice, like quality, defies definition since what may be viewed to be effective in one context may not be seen as appropriate in another. So, for example, in Denmark it is common practice to put babies to sleep in an unheated area, whilst in the UK this might be questioned, or the practice by practitioners of picking children up, which is commonplace in the UK, may be seen as inappropriate in a French nursery, where such closeness may be considered less necessary.

In describing effective practice, the *Birth to Three Matters* Framework (DfES 2002) implicitly outlines some aspects of quality. These can be found in the principles of the Framework and relate to the value placed on the centrality of parents' involvement in their child's well-being; the importance of relationships, especially that of a key person for the child; and the notions that children are individuals who develop in their own way; and that learning is a shared process between the child, the environment and the people they encounter. Assessments of quality can be based around much wider distinctions than this, some of which we will now discuss.

Children and parents matter

Whatever definition of quality is used, the most important measure, and the one that is of greatest significance in children's lives, is the judgements parents make, on their children's behalf, about whether a setting is suitable or unsuitable for their needs. That is, assuming parents are in a position to choose. Given the choice of a variety of settings, free from economic and access constraints, it is likely that most parents would choose to place their children in a daycare setting where they, and their children felt at ease safe and accepted. This suggests that uppermost in determining quality here is the ethos of the setting, and the intangible web of relationships that operate to ensure that service users are welcome, in reality, rather than merely as they are expressed in policy documents.

Young children are vulnerable and rely on adults to know, meet and communicate about their needs. The importance of this cannot be stressed too heavily since it is only through knowing children well that adults can begin to identify and then meet children's needs. Parents know their children very well. They know about their lived experiences, their ways of communicating, their culture, their likes, dislikes, their health, their development and their anxieties. This knowledge may remain tacit, unless and until the key people in the nursery begin to listen to, and talk with, a child's parents so that what is known by them becomes shared knowledge.

As knowledge about a child is shared in a respectful way, value is placed on what parents know and this contributes to creating an ethos of acceptance and trust between the family and the daycare setting.

Relationships matter

Relationships matter in any situation, but most of all in daycare settings where many children spend a substantial number of their waking hours. Children are, at the same time, creators, absorbers and reflectors of experience and tune into the subtleties and complexities of feelings, picking up emotions and expressing or retaining them in a variety of ways. At the same time, children carry with them from home a knowledge about relationships, which may not be reflective of what they encounter in daycare, but which may change as they discover how relationships are conducted in the daycare setting. For practitioners, then, the puzzle that must be unravelled is how relationships can be negotiated and promoted that support both the child and the family, since people relate in many different ways, especially when families may speak different languages, have different beliefs about childcare and have different ways of showing their feelings.

Birth to Three Matters (DfES 2002) offers support for practice on the card Healthy Choices by suggesting that practitioners may involve themselves in: 'Discussion and information-sharing with parents whose home language is not English [which] takes time but is essential'. It reminds us, on the card for Emotional Well-being, that 'Valuing children's race, cultural identity and gender by choosing appropriate resources, activities and experiences, increases their sense of belonging and contributes positively to their sense of well-being' (DfES 2002).

The nature of relationship(s) both defines and prescribes the nature of children's (and parents') experiences in daycare. A child's development does not rely solely on their physical needs being met, but is influenced greatly by the degree to which their emotional and social needs are met as well. The way parents feel they have been treated by practitioners not only influences how the parent feels but will indirectly impact on the way their child experiences the situation, since the dyadic nature of parent–child relations feeds both forwards and backwards: parent happy – child happy (usually); parent unhappy – child unhappy (sometimes).

Environment matters

The role of the environment in determining quality has been well documented (Bredekamp 1987; Penn 1997). However, as we have indicated previously, it remains questionable whether quality measures are sufficient for gauging particular aspects of daycare. For example, the availability of a seating area in a setting can be judged – in terms of its accessibility, its appropriateness, its comfort and so on – whereas what cannot be measured so easily is whether parents feel comfortable in using it; or whether it is a relaxing place, or one that everybody feels able to use. This is the point at which the ethos and the environment intertwine.

The environment, then, is more than simply the planned space in the setting, it is everything that is encountered from point of entry to the setting to point of departure. It also includes the resources in the setting; the images that are promoted; and the messages that these convey about what the setting is about. These signals may not be immediately obvious and different people will respond to them in different ways. They may indicate that the home languages of many are valued, or they may convey, albeit unintentionally, that some skin colours or races are of greater worth than others, since they receive 'more coverage'.

In Reggio Emilia, a region in northern Italy famous for its high-quality childcare provision, the environment has been described as the 'third educator' (Edwards et al. 1995). It is argued that in order for the environment to act as an educator for the child it has to be flexible: it must undergo frequent modification by the children and staff in order to remain up to date and responsive to their needs' (Edwards et al. 1995: 148). The contribution the environment makes to the child's experience should then not be underestimated since when it is operating at its highest level, as described, it can provide a backdrop against which the scenarios of daycare can be played out very favourably. In describing ways of meeting the diverse needs of children and families *Birth to Three Matters* (DfES 2002) states, on the card Being Acknowledged and Affirmed, 'An inclusive environment is one which involves parents and the local community in ensuring that resources and activities are respectful of diversity', and on the card for Representing 'Symbols and pictures which represent home experiences, language and culture help children recognise they are valued and recognised'. So the environment is dynamic, constantly changing to reflect different children, different families, different practitioners.

Quality matters out of doors

The environment is as much about the outdoor space as about the space within the building. Children frequently find themselves restricted from exploration and discovery by the measures intended to keep them free from harm. Again, much has been written about what constitutes a quality outdoor environment (Bilton 1998; Ouvry 2000), though nothing can yet measure the way the environment is managed to support children's independence and mastery, or the ways practitioners can understand risk assessment procedures yet still support babies and young children to take risks and to be exploratory. So whilst there is an increasing emphasis on provision of quality outdoor areas for babies and young children, maximizing their use is a subject that is worthy of greater consideration.

What is quality out of doors for a Heads Up, Looker and Communicator (birth to 8 months old), or a Sitter, Stander and Explorer (8–18 months old), or a Mover, Shaker and Player (18–24 months old), or a Walker, Talker and Pretender (24–36 months old)? Is it the same, or different, for each child? Is it the same or different for children in the same age group? Should the younger babies and the older children mix, when one group may be mobile, whilst the next may not? How can we get round the thorny issue of England's weather so that we can ensure the environment is accessible at all times, with the exception of extreme and unusual conditions? Obviously the answers to some of these questions are as various as the care contexts in which children are placed and every setting will have an individual approach to how they group and organize children at different times of the day and how they decide whether children are to go out of doors if it is wet, or windy, just as the nature of the outdoor space will be defined by the location and purpose of the setting.

Childcare settings are based in many situations. Whatever outdoor space is available to a setting it is important to capitalize on the best of what is on offer to ensure quality outdoor provision. For example, the *Birth to Three Matters* Framework (DfES 2002) suggests, on the Component card for Growing and Developing, 'Outdoor exploration and testing of physical abilities is important for all children. A sensitive, supportive adult can help children experience and achieve pleasure and control in sensations and movement'. This returns to the interface between the environment and relationships; the former is not sufficient without the latter. The way practitioners mediate children's experiences of the outdoor environment is an issue for all young children, especially those with disabilities, of whom the Framework reminds us 'When other children are climbing, exploring and running, a child with a physical disability may become frustrated and will require sensitive adult support, additional resources or adaptations to equipment'; whilst it also implies that adults are responsible for ensuring children develop a sense of danger. Allowing children open access to outdoor space will ensure that they develop a sense of danger, since experience is one of the ways children learn about risk.

Planning matters

Planning for children's experiences in daycare has become an increasing concern for practitioners, parents and inspectors, as well as all those who are interested in supporting continuous improvement both in schools and childcare settings. The benefits of planning in care and education have been discussed in many publications and, more recently, discussion has focused on what planning might look like for babies and young children (Bruce and Meggitt 1999; Post and Hohmann 2000). To plan is to prepare, to make ready, to consider beforehand, and undoubtedly is a requisite for work with young children. However, if planning is to be appropriate it should have 'fitness for purpose' and provide open-ended opportunities for children's developing interests and preoccupations, rather than a straitjacket, restricting experiences and driving adult involvement. There is a very fine line, however, between the two, and any planning should be based on clear principles and understandings about young children's characteristics and needs. The following principles, taken from the *Birth to Three Matters* Framework (DfES 2002), are noteworthy in relation to this:

- Learning is a shared process and children learn most effectively when, with the support of a knowledgeable and trusted adult, they are actively involved and interested.
- Children learn when they are given appropriate responsibility, allowed to make errors, decisions and choices, and respected as autonomous and competent learners.
- Children learn by doing rather than by being told.
  (DfES 2002)

Implicit in these principles is a view of learning that is grounded in warm and supportive relationships; that is based on the child's interest in what is to be learned; and that builds in opportunities for trial and error, decision making and active involvement. Planning for these processes is complex and individualistic and requires skill and sensitivity on the part of the practitioner and sound evidence drawn from observation of the child and evaluation of the provision. In principle this should be a straightforward process, in practice planning is sometimes driven by views of what will be said when 'an inspector calls'; in other words practitioners frequently feel that planning is a paper exercise that must be completed and that practice must follow what has been described.

We would argue that planning for young children should be flexible – should flow with the child and may often be written retrospectively to describe and reflect on how what was planned followed a particular 'avenue of exploration'[1] since the purpose of planning for babies and young children is not the demonstration of a particular practitioner's skill at crystal ball gazing. Rather, it is an endeavour to project into how any child might be expected to engage with materials, activities and experiences through the involvement of a skilful and sensitive adult. The importance of this approach cannot be understated.

Inspection matters

That inspection matters has traditionally been a cause of contention in both schools and nurseries in the past. However, more recently there has been an acceptance that, whilst sometimes unwelcome, inspection can have positive outcomes, particularly if it is linked to ongoing self-evaluation and development planning.

Where inspection has been less welcome, concerns expressed by practitioners working with very young children frequently relate to a lack of knowledge and experience of this age range on the part of inspectors. This is a particular concern in settings inspected as part of a combined inspection, or as a 'stand alone' nursery education inspection, when an inspector's early years experience might not be extensive. Those inspecting under the *National Standards for Under 8s Day Care and Childminding* (DfES/DWP 2003) may have worked with 3- to 5-year-olds, but their experience of children below this age may be limited. It is clear that for both these groups an understanding of the *Birth to Three Matters* (DfES 2002) materials will be important, not only in helping them to understand babies and young children, but in supporting them in inspecting settings in which the *Birth to Three Matters* Framework (DfES 2002) already plays a central role in planning and provision.

Also, the time allocated to the training of inspectors is short, and materials that provide information and challenge long-held views about the needs and capabilities of young children are important in ensuring that the inspection process makes a positive contribution on the quality of provision and practice in early years settings.

There is also a concern that, for settings in which combined inspections take place, there is some disparity between the focus of the two regimes. In daycare settings inspectors are largely interested in care and health and safety issues, as outlined in the *National Standards for Under 8s Day Care and Childminding* (DfES/DWP 2002), and only Standard 3 focuses fully on play and learning. On the other hand, it could be argued that there is an overemphasis on the curriculum, as opposed to the child, in requirements for the inspection of Nursery Education (S122), and that the wider issues which lead to children becoming strong and emotionally healthy can sometimes be overlooked.

The philosophy and ethos of *Birth to Three Matters* (DfES 2002) and the *Curriculum Guidance for the Foundation Stage* (QCA/DfEE 2000) purport to be the same, yet there are clear differences in priorities. Although in theory it should be easier for settings providing for babies and children from birth to 5 years to offer experiences that are 'seamless', in practice a different regime often exists for children over the age of 3 years. Similarly, there are two distinct purposes of inspection and each makes assessments of quality in relation to very different criteria. It is not then surprising that, to the uninitiated, their ratings can give rise to some confusion.

As indicated in Table 6.1, in the National Standards, there are three judgements or assessments which are fairly self-explanatory: 'Good', 'Satisfactory' and 'Unsatisfactory'; whilst the Nursery Education terminology refers to 'Acceptable' and 'Unacceptable' provision, though the former carries a number of provisos in relation to the levels of acceptability – that is, whether it is of high quality, of good quality or has some significant areas for improvement. The latter judgement appears to be somewhat incompatible alongside the term 'quality', suggesting an inadequacy of the available terminology.

Table 6.1 How quality is described in the two inspection regimes

National Standards	S122 Nursery Education
	Acceptable:
	High quality
Good:	Acceptable:
Goes beyond the standards	Good quality
Satisfactory:	Acceptable:
Meets the standards	Has some significant weaknesses
Unsatisfactory:	Unacceptable
Does not meet the standards	

Whilst quality is associated with effective communication, integrated provision and joined-up services, there is still some way to go in bringing this about in all areas of work with young children. The inspection process is one such area. The appointment of the right people as inspectors, provision of appropriate training and recognition of the important role they play is a significant move towards making the system more effective.

Proposals for an integrated framework for the Inspection of Children's Services in England, under consideration as we write, are welcomed by all those who share the concerns outlined above. The aim is to reduce unnecessary separate inspections of individual services and to facilitate multi-agency working. The outcomes of such integration will also no doubt eradicate the confused terminology in use at present, as well as streamline the inspection process, ensuring that consistent criteria are used across a number of settings.

Developed in the light of the Green Paper *Every Child Matters* (HM Treasury 2003), the inspection document has been drawn up by a Steering Group comprising the Office for Standards in Education (OFSTED), the Audit Commission, the Healthcare Commission, the Constabulary Inspectorate, and several other commissions and inspectorates linked to various key services. Discussion with councils and other stakeholders will ensure that as wide a range of views as possible is sought via national and regional conferences. The document, subject to the passage of the Children's Bill, marks a

significant move towards the collaboration and coordination of services advocated by the early pioneers of multi-agency developments (DES 1990).

David Bell, Her Majesty's Chief Inspector of Schools (HMCI), who acted
as Chair of the Steering Group for the integrated inspection framework,
speaking at a stakeholders' conference, stated that:

> For children's services to be effective and efficient their objectives
> have to be better integrated and their actions ... better co-ordinated.
> So, the proposals for an integrated inspection framework have the
> intention that all inspectors of children's services, where relevant
> will report on their outcomes for children and young people in a
> systematic way.
>
> (Bell 2004: 1)

Whilst quality is clearly to be endorsed, only when there is synergy between
services can the best outcomes for service users be guaranteed. Ensuring a
joint approach to inspection is, then, as we write, much more than a hope, it
is now a welcome expectation.

Conclusion

As indicated earlier, quality is an elusive construct, which is transformed and
re-shaped by the perceiver and, whilst measures of its visible aspects are
possible, other features are both difficult to identify and, in some cases, immeasurable. How, for example, does one measure a welcoming atmosphere;
challenging experiences; the extent to which diversity is understood and
celebrated, and so on? It has been argued that an objectivist approach fails to
identify sufficiently the immeasurable nuances of an environment such as the
ethos, whilst relativist approaches leave any assessment bound by individual
perceptions and time. The conclusion we must reach is that whilst relativism
is dangerous, so too is objectivism, since neither is able to wholly reflect the
experiences of the participants – babies, young children, practitioners, parents and families.

What we do believe, however, is that quality is greater than the sum of its
parts and that it should derive from the will of all those involved in providing
childcare to offer the best that they can to enhance and enrich the lives of
very young children. Currently this willingness is high as practitioners embrace the *Birth to Three Matters* Framework (DfES 2002) in their quest for
quality at the present time. It seems, therefore, that a more comprehensive
approach to ensuring quality must involve all the stakeholders, not only
parents, children and practitioners, but also policy makers and quality teams
such as development workers and advisory teachers. In this approach the

views of all involved would be gathered so that a multiplicity of views is identified, shared, discussed, questioned, challenged, evaluated and agreed, through a process of self and organizational evaluation which would be validated both internally and externally. Whilst this process is likely to be lengthy and time-consuming it would reduce the possibility that one person, with a limited view, or another, whose view was tinged by looking through 'rose-coloured' spectacles, was not the sole contributor to a setting's practice being graded as either 'Acceptable' or 'Unacceptable' in relation to both a complex organization and its relationships as judged through narrow sets of criteria.

So, if quality issues are to be broadly addressed in work with children it seems that these should reflect particularly the views of parents (beyond the present completion of a form at around the time of inspection). Where assessments of the environment are made, these should derive from research with service users such as children and their families, rather than from the perspective of an outsider whose views about an environment may be inaccurate, or from the views of a practitioner calculating how they think parents may feel about a particular issue.

Outdoor environments are places where babies and young children are learning about the wider world, and assessments of these spaces should not only judge the extent to which they are safe but should also reflect how they provide challenge and promote adventure and exploration, even for the youngest children. Assessments should be based on the use of research methods that give access to children's views as well as those of adults.

In identifying quality in relation to planning, the focus should be on the extent to which what is planned is reflective of the needs, characteristics and interests of the individual child, rather than of groups of children, or the current theme or topic.

Inspection is a necessary process, which regulates and maintains careful records on the suitability of provision and practice in relation to children's care and education. Any convergence of the inspection regime that creates clarity about judgements is to be welcomed. However, what would, in our view, be more welcome is a process of inspection which fully involved and engaged stakeholders in a collaborative evaluation of early years education and care, with judgements derived from joint decisions between inspectors and inspected.

Finally, we would argue that quality is neither some unattainable holy grail, nor something that once captured can be preserved. Quality is dynamic and will change as new information emerges alongside new technologies, new policies and new kinds of childcare and childcare professionals. Innovative approaches to work with young children will always push the boundaries of what we perceive to be 'quality'. The challenge for all those involved in extending these boundaries is how we can truly reflect the views of all those whose 'voices' are not usually heard in examining, describing, evaluating and judging what is of 'quality' in early years contexts.

Note

[1] Thomas Coram Early Years Centre uses this term to describe a child's interests.

References

Bell, D. (2004) Talk given to Stakeholders Conference on Integrated Plans for Inspections, May, reported in *Nursery World*, 20 May.

Bilton, H. (1998) *Outdoor Play in the Early Years: Management and Innovation*. London: David Fulton.

Bredekamp, S. (ed.) (1987) *Developmentally Appropriate Practice in Early Childhood Programs Serving Children Through Birth to 8 Years*. Washington, DC: NAEYC.

Bruce, T. and Meggitt, C. (1999) *Child Care and Education*, 2nd edn. London: Hodder and Stoughton.

DES (1990) *Starting with Quality*, report of the Committee of Inquiry into the Quality of Educational Experience Offered to Three and Four Year Olds. London: HMSO.

DfES (2002) *Birth to Three Matters*. London: DfES Publications.

DfES/DWP (2003) *National Standards for Under 8s Day Care and Childminding*. London: DfES/DWP.

Edwards, C., Gandini, L. and Forman, G. (1995) *The Hundred Languages of Children: The Reggio Emilia Approach to Early Childhood Education*. Norwood, New Jersey: Ablex.

HM Treasury (2003) *Every Child Matters*, the Green Paper. London: The Stationery Office.

Moss, P. and Pence, A. (1994) *Valuing Quality in Early Childhood Services*. London: Paul Chapman Publishing Limited.

Ouvry, M. (2000) *Exercising Minds and Muscles: The National Early Years Network*. London: HMSO.

Penn, H. (1997) *Comparing Nurseries*. London: Paul Chapman Publishing.

Post, J. and Hohmann, M. (2000) *Tender Care and Early Learning*. Ypsilanti, Michigan: High Scope Press.

QCA/DfEE (2000) *Curriculum Guidance for the Foundation Stage*. London: QCA/DfEE.

Siraj-Blatchford, I. and Wong, Y. (1999) Defining and evaluating 'quality' early childhood education in an international context: Dilemmas and possibilities, *Early Years*, 20 (1), autumn.

7 Anti-discriminatory Practice Matters

John Powell

Introduction

John Powell's wide experience across many disciplines, his particular knowledge and commitment to anti-discriminatory practice, and his interest in babies and young children from birth to 3 ideally equip him to share his views on this important issue.

Very young children represent one of the least powerful groups in society and have no real way to resist any discrimination and prejudice that they may experience and which may have a devastating impact on their lives.

Early childhood practitioners are at the forefront of caring services, having regular and significant involvement with children and their families. This contact puts them in a strong position to intervene positively and make a real difference in children's lives.

The chapter will discuss how prejudice and discrimination operate interpersonally, communally and socially on children because of their diverse identities, which should be the cause of celebration, but which also offers opportunities, for some, to apply differential and negative treatment.

The chapter will argue that it is vital to develop anti-discriminatory practices that identify and challenge covert and overt prejudice and discrimination and will indicate practical ways that can be developed to support early childhood practitioners to help them to feel confident in this key area of work.

Developing the strong and healthy child

This section will refer to how children may develop to be 'strong' and 'healthy'. The *Birth to Three Matters* Framework (DfES 2002) introducing A Strong Child emphasizes that:

> At the core of A Strong Child lies the development of the baby's and young child's sense of personal and group identity and the ways this

can be acknowledged and affirmed by those around him/her. Identity is an intricate combination of characteristics, traits, features and behaviours. Together they contribute to a child's individuality, as well as their belonging to a particular cultural, racial, gender and social group. Identity is not static.

(DfES 2002)

The above reference raises some important concerns about the ways that children develop insights into who they are and where they belong. Babies and young children are also able to perceive whether or not they are approved of and what their membership of cultural, racial, gender and social groups means in the wider community. Practitioners and carers who are in contact with babies and young children on a regular basis have an important role to develop personal and professional awareness of the ways that they refer and relate to children in their care. They will be able to construct children as diverse, rich beings who should be part of an inclusive community by progressively developing practices that lead to the treatment of all children with respect. The practices that may follow from this way of constructing children as 'strong' and 'healthy' and part of an inclusive community require the practitioner to develop a relationship not just with the child but with the idea that children are representative of a rich inheritance of diverse characteristics which enhance social groups and influence the ways that the wider society operates.

Constructing the characteristics of babies and young children

The ways that individual characteristics of babies and children are socially constructed may be seen to operate on several levels. First, within the caregiving unit which I will refer to as the family, a baby often offers a symbolic focus for hopes, dreams and desires of caregivers and as such can represent a symbolic repository for stories from the caregivers' life-histories and the extensive range of expectations likely to be contained there. In other words, the expected child will be the subject of a set of social constructions that surround the awaited birth and which are connected to family memories of the experiences of carer practices that filter through to the new family via family members. This overlay of folk memory and parenting expertise presents a formidable set of expectations, not only for babies and children but also for new parents to be compared against. 'We need to allow that babies are born into a socially constructed location. Typically their caregivers bring to the "expected" neonate both a general culture and (often a more specifically instructed) knowledge of babyhood' (Stainton Rogers and Stainton Rogers 1992: 125).

Caregiving contexts including families and other forms of childcare provision such as childminders will tend to reflect a range of cultural values and concerns. Each context's understanding of what constitutes good practices will tend to make a significant impact on the parents and care providers and the new baby. Within most caregiving contexts there is a potentially wide range of insights into what constitutes competent parenting skills as well as others that are concerned with constructions of the child and child–carer relationship. The construction of care practice in the family unit may also be linked to anecdotal evidence passed from one generation to the next and which may help as additional sources to develop judgements concerning caregivers' apparent competence. In addition to the kinds of constructions mentioned above, there may be social expectations connected to a baby's gender or social class. These expectations may be connected to both a wider family and societal view of what constitutes appropriate behaviour from the caregivers and the baby. In some contexts the baby is watched to see if they reveal any clear indications of being special, such as whether they are advanced in their cognitive or social development. Debates can sometimes become heated regarding the interpretation of the responses of babies to their new world through small details such as facial gestures and what counts perhaps as a smile or the early formation of language. If a child is considered to have smiled or made a meaningful utterance at a very early age it may be that expectations are heightened so that further evidence of being more developed may be sought. This may result in the very youngest of children being constructed as 'intelligent', or if signs like these are less forthcoming the opposite may be believed.

The developing construction of the child

The 'gaze' of carers as it is directed to babies from the moment of birth shows a powerful adult agenda at work, observing and determining the meanings of early characteristics and how they might develop. Thinkers such as Foucault describe this level of observation as a form of 'disciplinary power' (Rabinow 1984).

The point that Foucault is making is that the expectations of parents, other family members, community members and caregivers through the practice of observing the behaviours and actions of babies and children are given meanings that reflect the values and beliefs present in the family or care unit and often in the wider society. This may also be argued to be the purpose of primary socialization operating through beliefs and values held by family and other carers. The baby and young child in this context may be seen to be entering a process of preparation for participating in the wider community. However, children may be seen also as 'active agents' (James et al. 1998) who are accomplished at picking up cues regarding these expectations and responding to them. In this sense babies and young children are personally engaged in their own development and as they become more aware of what is expected they may develop ways of anticipating what seems to be required of them.

Stainton Rogers and Stainton Rogers (1992: 126) also remind us that babies are about the future and its associated expectations. Sets of expectations relating to 'becoming' that are often constructed in the family and care unit and invested in the child may also relate to wider societal discourses such as education and health, and are often concerned that children will grow to be 'healthy' and 'intelligent' beings able to be contributing members of the wider society by meeting a range of personal and public challenges.

The family care unit may not always present the kind of opportunities that it claims it does. Although we make claims that what we are doing is good for children, this may not always be the case. Parents and carers are very powerful figures in the lives of young children and are constantly involved in making decisions about what is in the child's best interest.

Knowing the child (and the caregiver)

The discussion has identified some of the issues that relate to practice found within different primary care units and their significance regarding the growing child. The construction of caregiving practices, through the use of local narratives, can be seen to be an important way of understanding the powerful purposes of observational practices operated by caregivers. However, whilst there are general care practices that have currency and recognition across different care units and contexts, the part played by local narratives is to place emphasis on and thereby give meaning to particular actions. Babies and young children are from before birth developing as active participants within these narratives.

Narratives may be seen as ways of understanding caregiving in which babies' and young children's actions are portrayed as significant or not. Narratives record a set of the personal characteristics and idiosyncrasies of children by their carers. Similarly they indicate what is perceived as competent, caring practice. Through narratives a child becomes known and reported on, in relation to the values and beliefs held in the family unit, for example as a 'real' boy or a 'feminine' girl.

We can see throughout the discussion that there has been a powerful process whereby personal differences are identified and incorporated into the anecdotes of family carers. These sets of differences are also unsurprisingly part of what tends to be noticed within the wider community. Here the placement of individuals into their apparent social groups represents a number of divisions. Payne points out that:

> When we talk about social divisions we mean those substantial dif-
> ferences between people that run throughout our society. A social
> division has at least two categories, each of which has distinctive
> material and cultural features. In other words, one category is better
> positioned than the other, and has a better share of resources because
> it has greater power over the way that our society is organised.
>
> (2000: 2)

These divisions suggest features of identity that individuals may have in common with each other and are instrumental in identifying members of the same groupings. It is in this way that aspects of similarity as they relate to gender, race or social class lead to crude sifting between individuals and their apparent relationship to identity. By the same token, 'others' are immediately known for their representation of difference, as each person understands it in relation to themselves.

The processes that have been discussed connect strongly to the Aspects of the *Birth to Three Matters* Framework (DfES 2002), particularly A Strong Child with its emphasis on the child's realization of their own identity through:

- growing awareness of self;
- realizing that s/he is separate and different from others;
- recognizing personal characteristics and preferences;
- needing recognition, acceptance and comfort;
- exploring emotional boundaries;
- feeling self-assured and supported;
- valuing individuality and contributions of self and others;
- having a role and identity within a group.

Children also develop confidence through becoming A Skilful Commu-nicator, especially through:

- gaining attention and making contacts;
- being with others;
- sharing thoughts, feelings and ideas;
- negotiating and making choices.

Belief in themselves as A Competent Learner also empowers a child, particularly through:

- finding out about the environment and other people;
- becoming playfully engaged and involved;
- imitating, mirroring, moving and imagining.

A Healthy Child describes the importance of children:

- being special to someone;
- being able to express feelings;
- developing healthy dependence and independence;
- becoming aware of others and their needs.

Children are developing an understanding about themselves and who they are through relationships and their continuing involvement with others. However, there is the possibility that the recognition of difference may lead on to the practices associated with unequal and unfair treatment such as discrimination and prejudice. Identities may be constructed from several different aspects of social division, including gender, race and ethnicity, social class, age, disability and sexuality. These are all important features of social divisions but there are many others that could also be cited, including 'childhood'. Jackson and Scott, in exploring the impact of social divisions, argue that 'Childhood is the only form of social subordination that is still romanticised as a state of freedom' (2000: 152). This raises questions about whether children may suffer from discrimination because of the ways that their identities appear to be constituted by categories of social divisions.

Children and discrimination

Thompson offers the definition of discrimination as 'the process [or set of processes] by which people are allocated to particular social categories with an unequal distribution of rights, resources, opportunities and power. It is a process through which certain groups and individuals are disadvantaged and oppressed' (2003: 82).

Thompson (2003) goes on to argue that discrimination operates at three levels, which he identifies as the personal, the cultural and the structural. Everyone has a set of personal beliefs, values and attitudes that they may have grown up with, which are reinforced by other individuals and groups, and which are likely to find overt expression occasionally but more often arise at a covert and discreet level. It is easy for carers to hold ideas about families and children that may be quite negative because they do not seem to belong to the same groups that they do, for example the children of immigrant families and asylum seekers can be viewed in an unfavourable light simply because they are different.

Stereotypes therefore play a significant role in developing and reinforcing discriminatory behaviour. If some individuals behave towards other people according to stereotype, then those 'others' are less likely to be seen as individuals but chiefly as constructions of 'otherness' through a process of personal prejudice. Thompson (2003) argues that social categories such as race, gender and class can be subjected to procedures of discrimination that include practices such as marginalization and stigmatization. These discriminatory practices can then develop into active forms of oppression that include sexism, racism and classism.

In addition to the personal and individual level at which discrimination may take place, Thompson (2003) also argues that it may operate at a cultural level. Cultural patterns of discrimination may be conveyed through the language that is shared amongst a particular group. This may rely on humour, which allows what is valued to be identified in a culture whilst at the same time making it clear what is feared and rejected. The use of jokes to make points against individuals and groups because they seem different is a frequent phenomenon. The exchanging of humorous stories of others as figures of fun and ridicule reinforce negative perceptions and group boundaries.

Developing anti-discriminatory practices

Referring to issues relating to racial identity, Dominelli (2002) suggests that children of mixed parentage usually have their racial identity simplified and are treated as black children in their encounters with the helping professions. Yet if they have a white mother, the family is treated as a white family by workers in these groups, and the black father is rarely taken into account.

There are some important lessons for all practitioners in these insights that Dominelli highlights and that are concerned with the ways in which a set of anti-discriminatory practices may be developed. The nature of identity is shown to be complex and therefore has the potential to offer points of connection across cultural barriers. Dominelli gives the example that some individuals may be both oppressed and oppressor and illustrates this as follows: 'A white working class woman might share the feeling of being oppressed as a woman with a black working class woman while simultaneously oppressing her on the basis of race' (2002: 46). Whilst there are moments of insight into the ways that carers may be sharing oppression, there are likely to be others when an interpretation and/or over-simplification of the identities of others emphasizes the urgency of being aware of these practices.

A systematic means of challenging discrimination must start with the practitioner becoming actively involved in a process of self-awareness by recognizing their own values and beliefs about aspects of social identity. It is important to develop a means of paying heed to the ways that carers as powerful practitioners relate to aspects of diversity and the ways of inter-preting the sense of 'otherness' that Dominelli (2002) refers to. This suggests that heightening personal awareness by developing a questioning attitude to personal views may then lead to the identification of emerging prejudices, which we can then challenge. This process may be described as the creation of a system of self-surveillance, where each practitioner is concerned about the ways that they represent themselves through their values and attitudes in professional contexts. As Leavitt (1995: 11) reminds us, 'the regulative norms of the day care centre are tied to the caregivers' beliefs about children's be-haviours and emotions, and their own roles as care givers'. Of course, this may apply to a range of contexts where childcare is taking place. Leavitt (1995: 11) argues that an emotional culture may be created by caregivers that directly relates to the values that are personally held by them. For example, Leavitt points to one context in which picking up a child was considered as 'spoiling' because she was 'constantly picked up at home'. This practice may become integrated as a part of the cultural expectation for young children who come into contact with that caregiver. The norm in this example appears to be one that excludes picking up as an acceptable practice, particularly with children perceived as 'spoilt'. If, however, picking up is seen as appropriate for 'unspoilt' children, a set of discriminatory practices may be initiated that can result in some children feeling less approved of than others.

Siraj-Blatchford and Clarke (2000) argue that practitioners should find out as much as possible about the family to enhance understanding. This approach seeks to be actively inclusive and is interested in encouraging par-ental participation as a way for practitioners and parents to share as many insights as possible about the experiences that children they are caring for have both in the home and in the care context. Children may be seen as representatives of diversity with varying cultural beliefs and practices that should be celebrated. This is an effective way to develop a set of practices that can regularly challenge stereotypical ways of thinking by welcoming the presence of diversity in the wider society.

This is also a position that needs to be adopted by institutions through training to support the development of positive practices and reducing boundaries that may lead to exclusion. From what has been argued earlier, anti-discriminatory strategies should be geared to personal, cultural and structural locations. Dalal (1994: 26) suggests specific questions should be asked, such as 'what play materials would you provide in a nursery environ-ment to encourage non-sexist/racist play?' and that staff should be en-couraged to think about how they would deal with a situation in which they heard one child saying to another 'I'm not playing with you because you are black!'

These are useful as focal points in offering opportunities to rehearse the ways that care staff may respond but could be made more interesting by inviting staff to share experiences when they have responded to potential prejudice and discrimination.

In the case study for the Component Growing and Developing, a programme of inclusion focuses on the opportunity to eat together. The activity allows barriers, possibly erected through processes of categorizing according to social divisions or emotional cultures that may lead to discriminatory practice, to be robustly challenged as parents and children share a meal of: 'carrot, pieces of fruit, raisins, sultanas, bread to be eaten with the fingers, alongside mashed potato, rice, stewed fruit, ice cream and other food to be eaten with a spoon' (DfES 2002).

During this type of activity children's social development may be actively engaged across a range of interactions that require listening and talking. Courtesy and turn-taking, and independence and improved confidence (Bruce and Meggitt 2002) and self-esteem will be enhanced as the child's family and cultural background are valued through sharing their mealtime traditions (Lindon et al. 2001).

Conclusion

This chapter has discussed the ways that babies and very young children are understood through narratives that identify their potential as well as judging areas in which their behaviour or development does not meet expectations. There has been an exploration of the part that social divisions play in determining, through a process of allocating categories as an everyday practice, the ways that discriminatory attitudes, values and beliefs may develop. To be anti-discriminatory in practice means to develop reflective insights into personal perspectives and to actively challenge them. It also means developing inclusive activities that allow for the development of understanding across cultural barriers as a means of breaking them down. Dalrymple and Burke (1995: 137) suggest that there are eight key elements leading to making the participation of the community a reality:

- resources;
- sharing information;
- training;
- research and evaluation;
- equal access and opportunities;
- forums and structures for involvement;
- language;
- advocacy.

These principles recognize the importance of inclusion through encouraging participation from all service users, so that their voices are included as an important part of the discourses framing childcare practices. They also emphasize the enormous possibilities present for developing insights and awareness into the complexity of diversity in the world that can be recognized through the eyes of children and their carers growing together.

References

Bruce, T. and Meggitt, C. (2002) *Child Care and Education*, 3rd edn. London: Hodder and Stoughton.

Dalal, P. (1994) in H. Eadie and P. Millar (eds) *Challenging Racism in the Early Years: The Role of Childcare Services in Scotland and Europe*, papers from a conference organized by Children in Scotland and Fife Regional Council. Edinburgh: HMSO.

Dalrymple, J. and Burke, B. (1995) *Anti-Oppressive Practice: Social Care and the Law*. Buckingham: Open University Press.

Dominelli, L. (2002) *Anti-Oppressive Social Work Theory and Practice*. Basingstoke: Palgrave Macmillan.

Jackson, S. and Scott, S. (2000) Childhood, in G. Payne (ed.) *Social Divisions*. London: Macmillan Press.

James, A., Jenks, C. and Prout, A. (1998) *Theorizing Childhood*. Cambridge: Polity Press.

Leavitt, R. (1995) The emotional culture of infant-toddler day care, in J. Hatch (ed.) *Qualitative Research in Early Childhood Settings*. Connecticut: Praeger Publishing.

Lindon, J., Helman, K. and Sharp, A. (2001) *Play and Learning for the Under Threes*. London: TSL Education Ltd.

Millam, R. (2002) *Anti-Discriminatory Practice, A Guide for Workers in Childcare and Education*, 2nd edn. London: Continuum.

Payne, G. (ed.) (2000) *Social Divisions*. London: Macmillan Press.

Rabinow, P. (1984) *The Foucault Reader*. London: Penguin.

Siraj-Blatchford, I. and Clarke, P. (2000) *Supporting Identity, Diversity and Language in the Early Years*. Buckingham: Open University Press.

Stainton Rogers, R. and Stainton Rogers, W. (1992) *Stories of Childhood, Shifting Agendas of Child Concern*. Hemel Hempstead: Harvester Wheatsheaf.

Thompson, N. (2003) *Promoting Equality, Challenging Discrimination and Oppression*, 2nd edn. Houndmills: Palgrave Macmillan.

8   Inclusion Matters

Julie Jennings

Introduction

In developing the *Birth to Three Matters* Framework (DfES 2002) it was considered important that links were made with other significant initiatives and developments taking place at the same time. The production of practical guidance for professionals working with young children with disabilities and their families was one such development. Julie Jennings, with her specialist knowledge in this field, was a member of the Working Group which produced the final document *Together from the Start – Practical Guidance for Professionals Working with Disabled Children (Birth to Third Birthday) and Their Families* (DfES/DoH 2003). She kept in close touch as the *Birth to Three Matters* materials were written and was a valuable consultant to the project team. In this chapter she focuses on inclusion.

Inclusion is currently high on the political agenda in a variety of forms and contexts. It is often defined in terms of its reverse: those at risk of social exclusion (see Sammons et al. 2003). Inclusion is an emotive term: it is a complex subject which engenders passionate debate and is open to wide interpretation. For a child under 3, inclusion starts in the home with the inclusion of the whole family. In this chapter, discussion relates specifically to the opportunities for inclusive education and care provided by the *Birth to Three Matters* Framework (DfES 2002). This is set in the context of special educational needs and disability – terms that will be used as they represent the current language of legislation – although many of the issues will encompass a wider concept of inclusion, such as ethnicity.

Introduction: the context of inclusion

One definition of inclusion states that it 'is a process of identifying, understanding and breaking down the barriers to participation and belonging' (Early Childhood Forum 2003).

This powerful declaration is deceptively simple, almost as simple as Baroness Warnock's (1986) statement: 'If I am to walk along a road, I need shoes; but there are those who need a wheelchair, or a pair of crutches, or a guide dog, or other things besides. These needs could be identified and met, and then off we could all go together.'

The *Warnock Report* (DES 1978) laid the foundation for more inclusive practices for children with special educational needs (SEN) and established the concept of a continuum of need. The report ultimately led to the publication of the *Education Act 1981* (House of Commons 1981), reaffirmed in subsequent Education Acts (HMSO 1993, 1996), which emphasized the right of all children with SEN to be educated alongside their peers in mainstream provision and to join in all activities in a collaborative way, wherever possible. Gilbert Mackay notes that 'a generation after the *Warnock Report* (DES 1978), there are signs that we may be about to address some of its more radical perspectives in the spirit in which they were written' (Mackay 2002: 159).

The key perspective is that **inclusion is a process**: it is not a finite state. Inclusion cannot be universal or absolute in its application: there are cultural and historical differences, which mean that our understanding of it evolves. Since the publication of the *Warnock Report* (DES 1978), our perception of disability is changing: a recognition of diversity and difference replacing deficit and compensatory models. Indeed, the usefulness of retaining the concept of SEN is being challenged (Jones 2000).

Bertram and Pascal (2002) indicate that inclusiveness is a core principle of several international early years curricula. The assumption underpinning Te Whariki (New Zealand Ministry of Education 1996) is that the care and education of children with special needs will be encompassed within the principles, strands and goals set out for all children in early childhood settings. Te Whariki is designed to be inclusive and appropriate for all children and anticipates that strategies will be incorporated which enable children to learn together in all kinds of early childhood education settings (New Zealand Ministry of Education 1996: 11).

Malaguzzi describes the Reggio Emilia approach – the 'listening pedagogy' or 'negotiated curriculum' of the Hundred Languages of Children – as a recognition of 'differences in the make-up of children along with differences that can be reduced or widened by the favourable or unfavourable influences of the environment' (Edwards et al. 1993: 73). Philips (2001) argues that the Reggio approach itself is inclusive: the curriculum, organization, teaching and learning styles all contribute to an inclusive ethos. Children are viewed as having 'special rights'. Indeed, in 1995 legislation covering the Reggio Emilia region established that disabled infants from birth to 3 years of age had a guaranteed place in the infant-toddlers' centres, even where there was a waiting list. These examples are useful to bear in mind when considering what this means for the development and learning of babies and young children through *Birth to Three Matters* (DfES 2002), which itself provides a useful conceptual model to support inclusion.

Development matters

An understanding of child development is essential for any early years practitioner. The heritage of pioneers of early childhood education has been to establish a bedrock or tradition of practice, as described by Bruce (1987, 1997) and others. Against this, new knowledge – for example, the emerging understanding of the complexities of brain development – is placed. Writers such as Gopnik et al. (1999) have used this emerging knowledge within their broader research to reflect on specific conditions like autism in which, as David and her colleagues recognize, 'development does not occur quite so readily' (David et al. 2003: 10) and may be less predictable.

There is no real evidence to suggest that the pathway of development for children with specific impairments is substantially and qualitatively different from that of other children, although the sequence and rate of progress along the pathway may vary and some of the behaviours they show us may differ. It is important, as Woodhead states, 'to recognize the plurality of pathways to maturity' (Woodhead 1991: 50).

Birth to Three Matters (DfES 2002) is helpful to parents and practitioners in this because it reaffirms the view that all children are competent and capable from birth, and – most importantly – it does not reinforce a 'milestones' approach to development. It describes broad areas, from Heads Up, Lookers and Communicators, to Walkers, Talkers and Pretenders, along which children can take their individual journey, recognizing that children's development is uneven and can embrace all four stages at one time, which Bruce (2003) has called 'dancing the developmental ladder'.

Consider Rose:

Rose is a 2½-year-old who has multiple complex needs. Paul, a practitioner, is playing with Rose, as part of an individual programme of visual stimulation to encourage her to look at and track a moving object. But Rose is learning much more.

Rose lies on her back on the floor of the nursery. She has a naso-gastric tube of which she appears unaware. Her key worker, Paul, kneels in front of her. He is holding her favourite toy: a red and gold tassel. Rose smiles with excitement and her legs flex. Yes, she has seen it! She watches it pass, temptingly close. With a great effort, she reaches up her arms to grasp the tassel. Her hands remain fisted, but she brings them together and she has got it! Rose gurgles in triumph. 'You caught it!' says Paul. A spasm makes Rose drop the tassel and she frowns in frustration. 'Again?' says Paul, and holds up the tassel in front of Rose. 'Do you want to play again?' Rose's breathing quickens and her legs flex again in excitement. And play begins again.

Initially it may appear that Rose could not be considered A Strong Child, A Skilful Communicator, A Competent Learner, or A Healthy Child, as exemplified in the four Aspects of *Birth to Three Matters* (DfES 2002). But let's look again.

A Strong Child: Rose has a growing awareness of self. She has personal preferences for the props she uses – the tassel – and is finding out what she can do in learning to follow, reach for and grasp it. She is gaining self-assurance through a close relationship with Paul, and feels supported.

A Skilful Communicator: Rose is understanding and being understood. She is communicating meaning through her movements, facial expressions and sounds, and is influencing others so that the play continues as she wants.

A Competent Learner: Rose is certainly making connections through her senses and movement; she is finding out about the environment and other people, and is playfully engaged and involved. In this way, she is understanding her world.

A Healthy Child: Although Rose has complex health needs, at this moment she is being special to someone and able to express her feelings of triumph and frustration. She is learning to gain control of her body and acquire physical skills, such as successful tracking of an object.

This is a successful learning experience for Rose in an inclusive setting. But does she feel included? Do the other children recognize that she is being included? It seems that inclusion is something that is often 'done to' young children. Young children notice differences in others and will ask questions: Why does Rose need that tube up her nose? Why does she need a special buggy? Why doesn't she sit up? But they do not place an absolute value or label on the differences and use these as the basis for excluding certain children from their play. They may get bored or frustrated with children who have special needs, if on occasions they do not play 'properly', within the rules that they have set for that activity, but that is not because their companions are blind or have cerebral palsy.

Katz (1993) suggests some basic questions to be asked from the point of view of a child in a childcare setting:

- Do I usually feel welcome?
- Do I belong?
- Am I usually accepted and understood?

In *Birth to Three Matters* (DfES 2002), A Sense of Belonging is a Component of A Strong Child and suggests ways of enabling children to acquire social confidence and competence. Children need to be where they feel that they belong. It is important that we try to ascertain children's views on this, particularly for very young children at an early stage of communication. This can be a challenge to practitioners, but there are examples of effective practice in this area (Dickins and Emerson 2004).

There are times when children need to be with children who are the same as them; there are times when they need to be with other children who are different from them so that they can try out a variety of roles in relation to their peers. Being with other children provides an opportunity to experience how others behave and to experience reactions to their own behaviour. This argument is rehearsed by Ivana Soncini in her interview with Cathleen Smith (1998), in which she puts forward the view that as a child, at times you declare who you are and what you are like, but other children will also tell you who you are. This is not to advocate that being with children with SEN is 'good for normal children' which is an often repeated contention, but that a healthy self-concept is based on knowing yourself and others through similarities and differences.

To support inclusion effectively, we need to develop our own understanding of the child and the child's own preferred strategies for learning. This is the approach to assessment that is the focus of the next section.

Look, listen, note

Margaret Carr outlines the shift in her views of assessment from a 'folk' model to a 'credit model, which is disposition enhancing' (Carr 2001: 11). The folk model emphasized deficit, using objective observation of skills reflected in a checklist approach. The much more complex parameters of her alternative model includes everyday practice; it is observation-based, requires interpretation and points the way to better learning and teaching.

This alternative approach to assessment is embedded in *Birth to Three Matters* (DfES 2002). It highlights things to observe and note as a basis for planning. It is a useful approach to evaluate the interplay of factors related to child, environment and disability. *Birth to Three Matters* (DfES 2002) suggests a focus for observations of children which provides a firm foundation for assessment based on children's true competency: 'when we plan for children, we base our ideas for activities and experiences on our knowledge of the children in our care'. Approaches to assessment of any child from birth to 3 years should embrace an understanding of the child within the family context. If children are not included in the early years, the whole family risks isolation and social exclusion. Parents are, indeed, key partners in effective practice.

Effective practice

This ethos is embedded within early years pedagogy; as evidenced in *Birth to Three Matters* (DfES 2002) 'parents and families are central to the wellbeing of the child'. Hewson and Sisson (1996) have described the benefits of inclusion for parents in terms of acceptance and understanding. Families seek a sense of belonging too. From birth, the needs of most children under 3 years will be met within the family setting, which then gradually reaches out into the wider community. But what if the diagnosis or suspicion of SEN disturbs this context? What if the first months of a child's life are spent in hospital with the prospect, maybe, of not coming home? Many disabilities are diagnosed at birth; for some children, diagnosis will be an evolving process and parents will have to face new information at different stages of their child's development; for others, there will be no known cause.

Much has been written about the potential effects on parents and families of the birth of a child with SEN or a disability. The first experiences of hearing this news can have a profound impact which may influence the way that parents are able subsequently to relate to practitioners. The *Right from the Start Template* recognizes good practice in sharing the news 'to ensure inclusive practice right from the start' (Right from the Start Working Group 2003).

The experience of having a child with SEN has been described by one parent as 'a devastating experience which stays with you for the rest of your life' (Newman 1999: 16). Others report that it is like getting on 'the conveyor belt of care'; families feel that they become 'public property'. Although much of the research has focused on mothers, as Whalley (2001) states '*parents* means fathers too' – and the family includes grandparents and siblings.

Most parents have a readily available context for understanding child development within their immediate family, or from sources such as magazines, or the library. But, as parents confirm, there is not an equivalent body of knowledge if your child is born blind, or with another disability. Kingsley (1987) has written emotively about her experiences in *Welcome to Holland* and she confirms that you need 'to go out and buy new guidebooks and learn a whole new language' when a child with a disability is born.

There are variations in family resources and in their responses to disability. As in other aspects of inclusion, there is always a different point of view, such as that advocated by Parents for Inclusion. In *Welcoming All Children into the World* (2002), they set out their vision for an ideal world where there is no:

- antenatal testing;
- prejudice;
- targets of 'normality';

- developmental checklists;
- brain grading;
- medical model of disability.
  (Parents for Inclusion 2002: 6)

This is a salutary reminder for anyone working with very young disabled children and their families not to make any assumptions about how parents may respond to the birth of their child or view the provision on offer. In *Collaboration, Communication and Co-ordination* Roffey (1999) highlights key factors that underpin parents' relationships with services, both early years and SEN, at this time. Consider the nature of a parent's response to her disabled child in the following case study: Component card Healthy Choices, *Birth to Three Matters* (DfES 2002).

Laura, a 2½-year-old with severe learning difficulties, explores a length of chain during heuristic play. She repeatedly pulls it back and forwards across her mouth, constantly watching the adult and checking her response. When viewing this sequence on video, Laura's mum explained 'I know why she keeps on looking at you, she's waiting to see if you will react like I do, and say "stop putting things in your mouth!"'

By viewing the video sequence with the parent, the adult was able to share this experience with the parent and to talk about what Laura enjoyed doing and her responses and choices.

Involving parents in their child's learning is key to partnership working in the early years. The following two sections will explore some of these issues.

Play and practical support

'Somehow, we have to ensure that children want to communicate, that there is someone to communicate with, that they have something to communicate about and that we teach them that communication is enjoyable and brings results' (Mittler 1988: 13). Compare this with the statement: 'All children have from birth a need to develop, learning through interaction with people and exploration of the world around them', *Birth to Three Matters* (DfES 2002). The latter is written about the care and education of children under 3; the former, about children with a range of communication difficulties, yet they are interchangeable in the view of effective practice that they offer. In both statements, the key elements of effective communication and learning are the value given to the relationship with a responsive adult and the strategies for supporting and extending experiences through a challenging and stimulating environment.

Much discussion of inclusion focuses on the nature of the environment: is it accessible or a barrier? Wilson states that a major goal is 'to remove or side-step the barriers to learning' that children face and she advocates, in conjunction with environmental accommodations, a focus on the development of skills relating to play, social interactions, and exploration of the environment (Wilson 1998: 1).

Young disabled children are more dependent on significant adults to make play situations meaningful and valuable to their growth and development. However, it demands great creativity on the part of the practitioner to support and extend their learning to generate moments of shared attention and shared understanding which are based on the child's particular learning style.

The practitioner needs to capitalize on 'teachable moments' which Wilson describes as 'a situation that arises naturally in unstructured or semi-structured situations that provide a special opportunity for teaching a concept or skill within the context of what just occurred' (Wilson 1998: 257). Working on the premise that the child can learn, however severe the learning difficulties, our challenge is to find out how the child learns best. We can then develop learning opportunities, which build on the child's strengths and interests and minimize the potential developmental risks, in what Ferrell has called a 'thoughtful and planned use of the time available to increase the chances for success' (Ferrell 2002: 30).

This is precisely the approach advocated in *Birth to Three Matters* (DfES 2002). It does not provide a definitive list of activities and resources, but gives examples of interactions and experiences, which highlight ways of responding appropriately to the developmental needs of the children observed. Consider the case study from the Component card Making Meaning, which highlights a 'teachable moment'.

Richard, a 2½-year-old, has an autistic spectrum disorder. He can say a few words in imitation of adults but doesn't use them spontaneously. Although his parents feel he understands much of what they say, he cannot express his own needs and wishes. Helped by the portage worker, he's been taught to point to things he wants in picture books.

His mum recently found him, alone in the kitchen, pointing at a cupboard. This suggests that Richard doesn't understand that communication requires a partner. He now has symbols or photographs of things he likes to eat and drink which he gives to his mother, father or childminder to indicate what he wants. In this way, he is able to communicate meaning more effectively.

However, it is important that practitioners are supported in their endeavours by specialists in the field, their colleagues and any relevant literature. The following section will outline the wider framework that is available for practitioners working with young disabled children and their families.

Planning and resourcing

There is a legal basis to meeting the special educational needs of children. The Education Act 1996 (HMSO 1996) and Special Educational Needs and Disability Act (HMSO 2001) set out the duties that local authorities have in relation to children whose needs require special educational provision to be made for them. Section 312 defines this as 'for children of 2 or over, educational provision which is additional to, or otherwise different from, the educational provision made generally for children of their age in schools maintained by the LEA, other than special schools, in the area; for children under-2, educational provision of any kind'. However, procedures for very young children are not specified in legislation, which may leave these children and their families vulnerable to variations in service provision. Two key documents give more detail on how the framework should work in practice:

- *The SEN Code of Practice* (2001) offers practical guidance on how to identify and meet the needs of children with SEN. It has a separate section for early education settings, which includes Early Years Action and Early Years Action Plus.
- The Special Educational Needs and Disability Act (HMSO 2001) extends the coverage of the Disability Discrimination Act so that it is unlawful for any provider of early years childcare and education to discriminate against any disabled child in the provision of any service.

Early years provision has expanded over the decades, but it has only recently come within the remit of SEN legislation and guidance, which has meant, of necessity, that the profile of SEN in the early years is rising (Wolfendale 2000a). This places extra demands on practitioners. In recognition of this, some recent guidance has focused on the needs of the youngest children and their families with an emphasis on early identification and intervention:

- *Together from the Start: Practical Guidance for Professionals Working with Disabled Children (Birth to 2) and Their Families* (DfES/DoH 2003), the principles of which are being put into practice through the DfES Early Support programme;
- *The National Service Framework for Children* (DoH 2004), which aims to

provide standards for all children's services, including those for young children with SEN or disabilities;

- *Every Child Matters* (HM Treasury 2003), which sets out proposals for reforming delivery of services for children, young people and families and which, along with *Every Child Matters: Next Steps* (HM Treasury 2004) informs *The Children Act 2004* (HMSO 2004).

The basis of all this government guidance lies in the common features of effective service provision, which have been summarized as follows:

- they provide a consistent, single point of contact for the family;
- they have a flexible, individualized, needs-led approach;
- they focus on parents' own concerns and recognize the importance of understanding parents' own perceptions of the hierarchy of their needs;
- support provided empowers parents rather than taking control away from them;
- parents' own expertise with regard to their child and family is recognized and acknowledged. (Sloper 1999: 95)

Such principles mesh with *Birth to Three Matters* (DfES 2002), which was developed alongside *Together from the Start* (DfES/DoH 2003).

Historically, intervention services for young children with SEN have focused primarily on the child, not the child in the family context. The ethics of intervention have been questioned (Penn 2000), not only in debates about medical intervention, such as the provision of cochlear implants for young children, but also in the very nature of working with families. Recognition is now given to the need for holistic, family-based support where parents have informed choice and a greater role in managing the services that affect them. Inclusive practice needs to be supported by inclusive integrated service structures. Health, education, social care and voluntary agencies are being challenged to work together with and for children and families in a more transparent, cohesive and ultimately inclusive way. Focusing on enabling systems of multi-agency collaboration, there is a resolution to push back the boundaries of inclusive practice. With this expectation must come a commitment to well-resourced training to support practitioner confidence in these new ways of working.

Meeting diverse needs

So what principles should underpin inclusive practice for children from birth to 3 years?

Mittler comments on research on the acquisition of pre-speech communication skills in normally developing infants that has been applied to children with severe learning difficulties: 'the lessons learned from a study of normal development are not strikingly new and may at first seem obvious. But it is only recently that we have begun to incorporate them into day-to-day work with children' (Mittler 1988: 11).

The 'lessons' of early years pedagogy which are embodied in *Birth to Three Matters* (DfES 2002) offer a framework for all children which acknowledges that babies and young children are social beings and competent from birth; that choices and opportunities should be provided which are meaningful to the child; that schedules and routines must flow with the child's needs; and that learning is a shared process and that caring adults count more than resources or equipment. These principles are fundamental to what *Birth to Three Matters* (DfES 2002) describes as 'providing for the very different needs of children'. Some of these children will remain 'very vulnerable', but still need to 'learn to be independent by having someone they can depend on'.

This is not to underestimate the profound impact of specific impairments which can put at risk a child's potential for learning: children with complex health needs may not feel well enough to engage in play activities; some may not be able to move independently to explore their immediate environment; some may not be able to choose from the range of activities that are available because they cannot see them; some children's behaviour may make it difficult for them to engage with other children; in particular, those children with life-limiting or regressive conditions challenge both parents and practitioners in their understanding of developmental progress, play and learning.

Birth to Three Matters (DfES 2002), like Te Whariki (New Zealand Ministry of Education 1996) and the Reggio Emilia approach, aims to be inclusive from the start. It offers children, parents and practitioners an exciting opportunity. Such interactive approaches which encompass the child, the social and physical environment and the nature of the SEN or disability, and that inform observation and planning, will enable practitioners to adopt a proactive approach to inclusion and will help to 'identify, understand and break down the barriers to participation and belonging' for children (Early Childhood Forum 2003).

However, inevitably the process of inclusion produces challenges and dilemmas for children, parents, practitioners and planners alike.

Challenges and dilemmas

Three 'matters' of inclusion that continue to pose challenges, dilemmas and questions for all involved in the care and education of babies and young children with disabilities concern the issues of:

- recognition versus labelling;
- equal versus differential rights;
- special education versus early childhood education.

Recognition versus labelling?

The vocabulary associated with inclusion poses the first challenge. The long-standing slogan of People First has been 'label jars not people', acknowledging that it is difficult to ensure inclusion 'without using terms which in themselves point to individual and group differences ... (and states). It is arguable that it is the word "special" which still maintains the deficit/medical paradigm as it differentiates them [children with disabilities] from other children' (Philips 2001: 58). This is also recognized in New Zealand, where children are identified 'who require resources alternative or additional to those usually provided within an early childhood education setting' (New Zealand Ministry of Education 1996: 11). There are echoes here of terms used in the SEN legislation in England, for example 'additional to or different from'.

Wolfendale comments on the language associated with SEN, which she calls a 'slippery, elusive concept', pointing out that 'distinct unease about such labels has pervaded practice too' (2000a: 3). Porter indicates that there has been a move away from diagnostic labels because of the stigma that they attract. However, she proposes that labels can be useful, especially to families, when they offer information 'by describing, explaining, and, at times, predicting the developmental progress of their child' (2002: 54). Labels may still be necessary in the current climate to ensure appropriate recognition for specific needs, as Mackay states 'Failure to recognise and failure to provide also lead to a failure to acknowledge disability as part of normal diversity ... Disability can disappear positively only when it is accepted completely as a part of normality. We have quite a way to go before that happens' (2002: 159 and 162).

Equal versus differential rights?

The second challenge follows on from this: recognition brings with it the responsibility to provide. To return to Warnock's analogy, if the wheelchair, crutches or guide dog are not made available, we are not going to get very far down the road together. Those resources, which are 'additional to or different from', may require a differential approach, not the same approach. This is a frequent confusion in discussions of inclusion and equality issues. This issue also impacts on the question of 'standards'. Should standards apply equally or do we regard individual progress in a differential 'value-added' approach?

This is a basic dilemma which Berry describes as 'the increasing demand for inclusive practices and educational opportunities for all children [which] appear to contradict and be in competition with policies focussed on raising academic standards and achievements' (2002: 160). How far and how soon will inclusion develop until individual children are respected for the progress they make in their own terms rather than progress against a decontextualized standard?

Special education versus early childhood education?

Behind this question lies a deeper challenge. There is historically a potential tension between the field of special education and that of early childhood education. Wilson states that 'a special challenge of the field is to merge these two disciplines in a way that retains the integrity of each' (Wilson 1998: 4). Wolfendale discusses areas of disparity in early years and special educational needs where she proposes that, both at local and national levels, 'there has been an historical separation of powers, interests and responsibilities' (2000b: 11). Hassan describes his struggle as a teacher of children with hearing impairment, feeling that 'the world of special education, a branch of education which has evolved its own separate identity and educational philosophy ... sits uneasily beside the nursery tradition' (1993: 36).

The argument has moved on in recent years and early years pedagogy, as evidenced in *Birth to Three Matters* (DfES 2002), offers a model of genuine inclusion to parents, practitioners and planners. At the same time, it acknowledges that working with babies and children is a complex, challenging and demanding task and that often there are no easy answers.

This chapter reflects evolving thoughts influenced by many people, children, parents, practitioners and colleagues, and represents a stage in my own learning journey. I have written elsewhere (Jennings 2002) that specialisms are necessary to support quality inclusion. In this particular context, the connection has been made between two specialisms: a broad vision of early childhood and a narrow focus on the exceptional needs of some children.

The fundamental challenge, it would seem, is that the process of inclusion is more about attitudes than systems of provision; it demands self-awareness and reflection. Robinson reminds us that in our relationships with children who have SEN: 'beliefs about and towards them, whether physical, social or emotional' are 'filters for our thinking' (Robinson 2003: 178). Inclusion is a most significant matter because it is a distillation of how we feel about others and ourselves. *Birth to Three Matters* (DfES 2002) offers another welcome filter for our thinking.

References

Berry, T.A. (2001) Does inclusion work? Simon's story, in C. Nutbrown (ed.) *Research Studies in Early Childhood Education*. Stoke on Trent: Trentham Books.

Bertram, T. and Pascal, C. (2002) *Early Years Education: An International Perspective*. London: Qualifications and Curriculum Committee.

Bruce, T. (1987) *Early Childhood Education*. London: Hodder and Stoughton.

Bruce, T. (1997) *Early Childhood Education*, 2nd edn. London: Hodder and Stoughton.

Bruce, T. (2003) *'Play Matters' Presentation* at Early Years Conference, Manchester Metropolitan University, June.

Carr, M. (2001) *Assessment in Early Childhood Settings: Learning Stories*. London: Paul Chapman.

David, T., Goouch, K., Powell, S. and Abbott, L. (2002) *Review of the Literature to Support Birth to Three Matters*. Nottingham: DfES Publications.

DES (1978) *Report of the Committee of Inquiry into the Education of Handicapped Children and Young People*. London: HMSO.

DfES (2002) *Birth to Three Matters*. London: DfES Publications.

DfES/DoH (2003) *Together from the Start – Practical Guidance for Professionals Working with Disabled Children (Birth to Third Birthday) and Their Families*. London: DfES/DoH.

DoH (2004) *The National Service Framework for Children*. London: The Stationery Office.

Dickins, M. and Emerson, S. (2004) *Starting with Choice: Inclusive Strategies for Consulting Young Children*. London: Save the Children.

Early Childhood Forum (2003) *Policy Statement: Definition of Inclusion*. London: HMSO.

Edwards, C., Gandini, L. and Foreman, G. (eds) (1993) *The Hundred Languages of Children: The Reggio Emilia Approach to Early Childhood Education*. New York: Ablex.

Ferrell, K.A. (2002) Promises to keep: early education in the United States, *The Educator*, July–December.

Gopnik, A., Melzoff, A. and Kuhl, P. (1999) *How Babies Think: The Science of Childhood*. London: Weidenfeld and Nicolson.

Hassan, D. (1993) Special educational needs in the early years: towards a personal classroom philosophy, *Early Years*, 14 (1).

Hewson, J. and Sisson, S. (1996) Parents prefer inclusion: the views of parents of children with special educational needs in one mainstream nursery school, *Early Years*, 17 (1).

HMSO (1993) *Education Act 1993*. London: The Stationery Office.

HMSO (1996) *Education Act 1996*. London: The Stationery Office.

HMSO (2001) *SEN and Disability Act*. London: The Stationery Office.

HMSO (2004) *The Children Act 2004*. London: The Stationery Office.

HM Treasury (2003) *Every Child Matters*. London: The Stationery Office.

HM Treasury (2004) *Every Child Matters: Next Steps*. London: The Stationery Office.

House of Commons (1981) *Education Act 1981*. London: HMSO.

Jennings, J. (2002) A broad vision and a narrow focus, *Early Childhood Practice*, 4 (1): 51–9.

Jones, C. (2000) *Values and Special Educational Needs in the Early Years: from Policy to Practice*, draft poster paper presented at the EECERA Conference, 29 August to 1 September, London.

Katz, L. (1993) Dispositions: definitions and implications for early childhood practices: perspectives from *ERIC/ECCE: A Monograph Series*. Illinois: Urbana.

Kingsley, E.P. (1987) www.nas.com/downsyn/holland.html

Mackay, G. (2002) The disappearance of disability? Thoughts on a changing culture, *British Journal of Special Education*, 29 (4): 159–63.

Mason, M. and Davies, A. (ed.) (1993) *Inclusion, the Way Forward: A Guide to Integration for Young Disabled Children*. London: VOLCUF.

Mittler, P. (1988) Foreword to J. Coupe and J. Goldbart (eds) *Communication Before Speech: Normal Development and Impaired Communication*. London: Croom Helm.

New Zealand Ministry of Education (1996) *Te Whariki Early Childhood Curriculum*. Wellington, NZ: Learning Media.

Newman, S. (1999) *Small Steps Forward: Using Games and Activities to Help Your Preschool Child with Special Needs*. London: Jessica Kingsley.

Parents for Inclusion (2002) *Welcoming All Children into the World*, unpublished consultation response.

Penn, H. (2000) What is normal?, in S. Wolfendale (ed.) *Special Needs in the Early Years: Snapshots of Practice*. London: Routledge Falmer.

Philips, S. (2001) Special needs or special rights? in L. Abbott and C. Nutbrown (eds) *Experiencing Reggio Emilia: Implications for Preschool Provision*. Buckingham: Open University Press.

Porter, L. (2002) *Educating Young Children with Special Needs*. London: Paul Chapman.

Right from the Start Working Group (2003) *Right from the Start Template*. London: Scope.

Robinson, M. (2003) *From Birth to One: The Year of Opportunity*. Buckingham: Open University Press.

Roffey, S. (1999) *Special Needs in the Early Years: Collaboration, Communication and Co-ordination*. London: David Fulton.

Sammons, P., Taggart, B., Smees, R., Sylva, K., Melhuish, E., Siraj-Blatchford, I. and Elliot, K. (2003) *The Early Years Transition and Special Educational Needs (EYTSEN) Project*, Research Report RR431. Nottingham: DfES Publications.

Sloper, P. (1999) Models of service support for parents of disabled children. What do we know? What do we need to know?, *Child: Care, Health and Development*, 25 (2).

Smith, C. (1998) Children with 'special rights' in the preprimary schools and infant-toddler centers of Reggio Emilia, in C. Edwards, L. Gandini and G. Forman (eds) *The Hundred Languages of Children: The Reggio Emilia Approach – Advanced Reflections*. New York: Ablex.

Warnock, M. (1986) Children with special needs in ordinary schools: Integration revisited, in A. Cohen and L. Cohen (eds) *Special Needs in the Ordinary School*. San Francisco, CA: Harper and Row.

Whalley, M. (2001) *Involving Parents in their Children's Learning*. London: Paul Chapman.

Wilson, R.A. (1998) *Special Educational Needs in the Early Years*. London: Routledge.

Wolfendale, S. (ed.) (2000a) *Special Needs in the Early Years: Snapshots of Practice*. London: Routledge Falmer.

Wolfendale, S. (2000b) Special needs in the early years: policy options and practice prospects, in B. Norwich (ed.) *Early Years Development and Special Educational Needs*, Policy Paper 3. Tamworth: NASEN.

Woodhead, M. (1991) Psychology and the cultural construction of children's needs, in M. Woodhead, M. Light and R. Carr (eds) *Growing Up in a Changing Society*. London: Routledge.

9   Safety Matters

John Powell

Introduction

In this chapter John Powell draws on his extensive experience as a social services worker, team manager in education welfare, and trainer of the next generation of early childhood practitioners to consider the needs that are central to young children developing as 'strong' and 'healthy' beings able to fully participate in the world. This concerns the importance of developing and maintaining positive environments to support young children and their families. He addresses recent social policy developments and their influence on child protection practices, as well as the ways that children are likely to be socially constructed. The discussion explores the consequences of inappropriate care for children, and childhood itself as a vulnerable time for babies and young children.

The Healthy and Strong Child – setting the context

The focus on providing children with a 'healthy' context in which to grow and develop has been part of the government's strategy in helping them to reach their optimum level of development. In order to do this it should be recognized that babies and young children have needs and rights, which should be supported by practitioners, parents and carers who are involved in close and affirming relationships in which children are highly valued. 'Health' in this context suggests a set of circumstances in which children and their adult carers are engaged in responding to each others' needs through a mutually respectful approach.

In characterizing A Strong Child, the *Birth to Three Matters* Framework (DfES 2002) recognizes that 'Both the significant adults and the physical environment have an impact upon children's developing sense of themselves and their group identity, their affective world and their relationships with others' (David et al. 2003: 19). Children may develop as 'healthy' and 'strong' when they are able to interact with their environment and those who are to be found there. The denial or reduction of opportunity to explore and engage within their environment may adversely impact on their ability to fully develop to their potential.

Insight into the ways that health can be understood is available from a number of perspectives, but only two will be discussed in this chapter. The first, taken from *Birth to Three Matters: A Review of the Literature* (David et al. 2003: 106–39), describes health in terms of six dimensions – physical, emotional, mental, social, spiritual and environmental. Each of these dimensions is seen as contributing to the health and well-being of the individual, none being seen as more or less important than any other. However, as Meggitt (2001: 9–10) suggests, each dimension is inextricably linked to each of the other dimensions, resulting in outcomes for health being influenced by multi-stranded factors such as preconceptual elements, genetics, lifestyle, housing, accidents, environmental factors and government policies.

The second, taken from *The Framework for the Assessment of Children in Need and Their Families* (DoH 2000a) describes (good) 'health' as a set of factors which impact on children in positive ways to support them so that they are able to prosper in a range of contexts. For children to thrive the framework identifies sets of needs that should be identified and appropriately met. These include:

> Growth and development as well as physical and mental well-being. The impact of genetic factors and of any impairment should be considered. [It] Involves receiving appropriate health care when ill, an adequate nutritious diet, exercise, immunisations where appropriate and developmental checks, dental and optical care.
>
> (DoH 2000a: 19)

This concept of 'health' is a holistic model that considers the necessary basic conditions to promote children's well-being. This framework presents children's needs, the meeting of which, it is argued, will lead to them becoming stronger and more confident. It incorporates within its terms of reference additional factors that recognize children as diverse and complex beings through the ways in which they are perceived and constructed by carers.

The Framework for the Assessment of Children in Need and Their Families (DoH 2000a) highlights that a 'healthy' child is more likely to develop in an environment that is consistently supportive and encouraging, recognizing the needs and rights of children as emerging through their membership of peer, family and other community groups, all of which contribute to a child's developing sense of identity. 'Critically important to a child's health and development is the ability of parents or caregivers to ensure that the child's developmental needs are being appropriately and adequately responded to, and to adapt to his or her changing needs over time' (DoH 2000a: 20).

For care practice to be considered successful, a clear focus needs to be in place that supports children, as active participants, engaging with significant others in the world and where developmental needs are given due consideration. Possible areas of tension may exist for carers which are concerned with maintaining this kind of relationship and issues that relate to assessing the potential risk that may be present in different childcare contexts. It is important to explore possible risk and how the practices associated with it may impact on children's self-confidence and esteem. It is equally important for carers to be able to support children about whom child protection issues arise and for whom appropriate intervention is necessary. The *Birth to Three Matters* Framework (DfES 2002) emphasizes the importance for practitioners of 'liasing with others where there are concerns about children's development, protection and welfare' (A Healthy Child: Keeping Safe).

Supporting vulnerable families

Following the death of Victoria Climbié in February 2000 and the subsequent inquiry and report (Laming 2003), failings were emphasized in the ways that care practitioners failed to liaise and intervene effectively. The Inquiry was informed that a range of services representing a variety of disciplines had not communicated or worked towards supporting Victoria and that this failure to act had directly contributed to her death. In describing the suffering and death of Victoria as 'a gross failure of the system', Lord Laming (2003: 4) stated that 'it is clear to me that the agencies with responsibility for Victoria gave a low priority to the task of protecting children'. The concerns raised by the Inquiry report led to the Green Paper *Every Child Matters* (HM Treasury 2003) which also outlines some of the broader policy requirements needed to support the most vulnerable children in society. It proposes action in four main areas:

- supporting parents and carers;
- early intervention and effective protection;
- accountability and integration – locally, regionally and nationally;
- workforce reform.

It is hoped that the effect of these policies will be to give children, parents and carers better-resourced local communities, which would act as a focal point for service provision. This approach should mean that the emphasis for support will not rely solely on intervention in, for example, childcare, but also on community programmes that operate as models for prevention as a part of a system of child protection. The strategy of supporting parents and carers includes a range of initiatives including:

- universal parenting services;
- specialist parenting support;
- compulsory action with parents and families;
- improving fostering and adoption services.

The roles of local services including childcare, early year's education, social care and schools means 'working more closely with parents to strengthen their understanding of how to help their child's development' (HM Treasury 2003: 41).

Community provision – a brief case study

The focus on Sure Start, early years and children's centres as a means of community support enables the development of preventative work with centre users. In an Early Years Centre in Stockport, Cheshire, practitioner initiatives have been promoted successfully that meet both the needs of babies and young children and importantly those of centre users. Through the work of the Health Visiting Service, a Feeding Group has been established for local mothers and their children where concerns about feeding difficulties are discussed. The issues that the feeding group are responding to relate to children's failure to thrive, the reasons for which are varied and complex and extend beyond those relating to weight gain and eating difficulties (Skuse 1993; Raynor et al. 1999; Taylor and Daniel 1999).

Meetings take place on a weekly basis at the Early Years Centre and mothers and children are usually referred there by their health visitor, GP, paediatrician or dietician. The provision is strongly multi-agency, being staffed by two family centre workers and two specialist health visitors at each session, and organized and provided by workers from health, education and social services. The group offers places for up to ten children from birth to 3 years together with their parents or carers. The group aims are to make mealtimes a sociable and enjoyable experience and to provide the opportunity for play, especially messy, tactile experiences with food and other play materials. During sessions there are opportunities for 'Direct work with children, for example, through messy play, cooking, and painting. Direct work with parents takes place with the aim of reducing their anxiety and stress and at the same time mutual support by parents is also promoted. Attachment behaviour is encouraged through baby massage, singing together and eating lunch together' (Beswick and Pendrill 2004: 15).

Results of the group have been very promising. Evidence from the evaluation report (Beswick and Pendrill 2004: 15) shows that during the period 2000 to 2003 (all referrals) of the children with concerns regarding growth who were discharged from the service had improved by crossing one or more centiles upwards. In addition, all of the children currently receiving the service are reported as maintaining or improving growth. Improvements were observed both in the home and group settings in the child's social, cognitive, emotional and behavioural development and parent–child interactions:

- children experienced different play and different food;
- children gained confidence and a sense of achievement;
- children cooperated better with other children and grew less shy. Some children's sleep patterns improved as a result of improvements in feeding and eating patterns.

The feedback from parents was very positive and it was clear that they had perceived this kind of intervention as supportive and helpful. The report's authors highlighted that mothers had identified their sense of isolation from family and carers before accessing the group and that the experience of attending had provided support for themselves and their child(ren) (Beswick and Pendrill 2004: 23).

It is clear from this example of community support that it is in line with current policy concerns that were mentioned earlier. The message from the report emphasizes that issues of feeding which can cause anxiety and feelings of failure can be dealt with discreetly, proactively and rapidly and be perceived by service users to be empowering, concomitantly offering greater safety to children. It would appear that this type of programme is already successfully addressing the aims of the *Birth to Three Matters* Framework (DfES 2002) to develop 'healthy' and 'strong' children and by doing so will help to increase parents' feelings of pride and success. This preventative approach is clearly preferable to the situation that may arise when child ill-treatment occurs and social work intervention is necessitated, risking the alienation of parents. This is not to say that social work intervention is unnecessary, it is clearly extremely important, particularly in situations where the parent is unwilling to attend a group like the one mentioned above.

Responding to concerns of ill-treatment

The role of practitioners working with very young children is a responsible and challenging one in relation to the issue of suspected child abuse. Close involvement with and observation of babies and young children at times such as bathing and changing can create dilemmas, as illustrated in the case study presented on the Component card Keeping Safe (DfES 2002).

Two-year-old Mary is from a large family in which her older brothers and sisters always help her, whether she is playing, getting dressed or eating. Since she is never allowed to express her needs, she has become very passive. She is very small and the older children at nursery love to try to pick her up. On Monday morning, after the children had been playing in the outdoor area, some marks on Mary's legs become apparent to Elsie, her key person, when she is changing her nappy. Elsie asks Mary about the bruises, and because she is in a hurry, rather than wait for an answer, she says to Mary 'Did they do it, when you were outside?' to which Mary turns her head away. On reflection, Elsie decided to pursue this with other staff. She talked to them to try to discover whether the marks on Mary's shins had happened at the nursery. No one had seen anything happen. Elsie noted the conversations and her concerns and, following child protection procedures, consulted the named person in her setting responsible for child protection issues.

There are clearly moments when the appropriate action is to refer concerns to the relevant agencies for them to consider whether the situation warrants further action. Children do suffer from ill-treatment, but this statement needs to be put in context. There are approximately 11 million children in the UK, 4 million of whom are considered as 'Vulnerable'; 300,000–400,000 identified as being 'In Need'; 53,000 are 'Children Looked After'; and 32,000 have their names on child protection registers (DoH 2000b: 3). More recent figures show that the trend for the number of children on registers is actually declining.

An initial concern for practitioners is recognizing when a child may have been ill-treated. Sudden changes in behaviour offer possible indications that children may have suffered ill-treatment. In this sense the youngest of children will be able to convey their feelings through their actions even when they may not yet have developed the ability to articulate that ill-treatment may have occurred. Powell (1997: 131) argues that 'the voice of a child may be silent or non-verbalized but still be recognized; it may represent a more rounded expression which can include play and non-verbal communication as well as verbal expressions of feelings'.

It is clear that children are invested with considerable rights that should protect them from significant harm, defined in the Children Act 1989 (HMSO 1989, see Section 31 (9)) as meaning ill-treatment or the impairment of health or development. Colton et al. remind us that there are 'four broad categories of abuse recognized internationally: physical abuse, emotional abuse, sexual abuse and neglect' (2001: 126). It is therefore vital for carers to be aware of the ways in which significant harm may occur as a manifestation of these defined categories.

Whenever carers and/or professionals have concerns about the well-being of a child it is extremely important for early reporting of concerns to take place. Early years professionals are very important, particularly in the early stages of child protection as they work closely together to establish a clear set of information suitable for assessing the levels of risk and concerns that may be around. The importance of proper communication across professional boundaries cannot be over-emphasized and should be accompanied by appropriate recording. Following the launch in March 2004 of the *Children's Bill* (House of Lords 2004), measures to develop a more effective child protection service have been put forward. They include:

- The creation of an electronic file on every child in the country, so that those at risk of abuse, neglect, deprivation, offending or poor school performance can be helped before they reach crisis point.
- Local authorities, the NHS and other agencies will be able to share information about any suspicion of abuse or neglect in the family.
- The bill includes powers to shake up local government, in a bid to improve accountability for children's services. An independent commissioner will be appointed to champion the rights of children and young people in national and local government.
- The commissioner could conduct inquiries into any cases they are concerned about, although the education secretary will be able to ask them to investigate specific cases relevant to national problems.
- The schools inspectorate Ofsted will set the framework for monitoring and inspecting children's services. The education secretary could order a joint area review of children's services by two or more of the following watchdogs: the Chief Inspector of Schools, the Commission for Social Care Inspection, the Commission for Healthcare Audit and Inspection, the Audit Commission, the Chief Inspector of Constabulary, the Chief Inspector of Probation.
- 'Hit squads' will be sent into social services departments that are failing to protect children.
- Private foster parents will be registered by local authorities to ensure they are suitable carers.

Balancing risk and promoting resilience

Even when practitioners and carers feel that the environment they provide for children is as supportive and safe as possible through the provision of stimulation and opportunities to develop, they should still guard against complacency. For instance, it is important for carers to strike a balance in not setting too rigorous limits that may stifle children's behaviour, due to their concerns about the levels of risk in society. This is a real dilemma since it exposes the tension between the needs that children have to develop as autonomous beings whilst at the same time remaining alert to the possibilities of risk to children in the community. One manifestation of this tension is the anxiety expressed by many practitioners and carers that children should be kept in constant view when they are playing outside. This view constructs children as vulnerable and liable to be preyed on by those in the community wishing them harm. This may appear to be an over-protective response to perceived risk which may be counter-productive to the aim of encouraging children who are able to develop with a degree of autonomy.

Parents and carers are frequently bombarded by media images of a world where those people who make up the very fabric of the local community are shown to be questionable and potentially pose a danger. However, as Richardson and Bacon (2001: 9) argue, 'a society where the main focus on abuse is the stranger, leaves children vulnerable'. The view that children are more likely to be ill-treated by those who care for them is put by Gibbons et al. (1995: 27), whose research findings indicate that 'the child's injury was inflicted by female caregivers in 40 per cent of cases; and by the male caregivers in 43 per cent'.

Tension exists for carers between seeing children in ways described in Rousseau's model of the child as a free spirit, which connects to aspects of late twentieth-century liberal constructions in which the child is encouraged in wandering and exploring their environment, and more protective anxieties that suggest that this type of activity is one loaded towards risk. James et al. even suggest that 'they must be allowed to go where their journeying takes them and they must be encouraged in their pioneering spirit' (1998: 38).

Children whose needs may be met through this more independent set of social experiences are perhaps likely to be less vulnerable and develop as more confident and assured and therefore less likely to come to harm. However, the need for children to develop in the ways referred to above is difficult when 'the concept of risk has become increasingly associated with negative outcomes: hazard, danger, exposure, harm and loss' (Douglas 1986, 1992; Parton et al. 1997). Culpitt argues that, 'lessening of risk, not the meeting of need' is at the heart of social policy (1999: 35). This view constructs risk as universal and something that needs to be reduced. However, this would seem to be a problematic project and one that, if successful, could undermine children's need to explore and make sense of their environment. In addition the act of surveillance that might accompany a rigid risk management approach would locate power and social control with adults and away from children.

Through the development of a range of contacts, young children may be perceived as being under the protection of caregiving and support networks of a community. There is, in such a context, the opportunity to develop a sense of resilience in children and reduce the perceived extent of risk to their well-being. Where children are able to initiate interactions and be seen as participants there is also a likely blurring between the boundaries that exist between adults and children. Whilst this blurring may be argued by some to be an important aspect of children developing their sense of social identity, others are likely to warn that this set of participatory practices, with a range of others in their community, contains risks of ill-treatment and abuse. This is where Sure Start Children's Centres and Early Years Centres can arguably be such a valuable resource in providing a safe but interesting and challenging environment for the youngest children. There is also the possibility that carers and parents will be able to meet in relaxed circumstances and discuss ways of improving the daily lives of children and their families.

Resilience ultimately may be viewed as a balancing of ideological sets of principles and practices that recognizes that children need to explore their environment, at the same time recognizing that there is always likely to be some form of risk. The challenge for practitioners lies in attempting to reduce risk without curtailing the activities of the children too drastically.

Jackson and Scott point out that 'risk anxiety has material effects. Parental fears can limit children's lives and experiences in a range of ways, thus increasing their dependence on adults' (2000: 16). The preparation of young children as confident explorers of their environments is something that may be developed through a positive and caring set of early relationships.

Discussing the ways that adults may respond to children in the nursery, Marsh (1994: 139), reporting on her research in a nursery, says that 'sensitive interaction between an adult and a child ... was often demonstrated by the adult sensing the child's need or potential unease and responding before the child became upset'. The point that Marsh makes is that practitioners who know their children well can be in the best position to support them if they seem insecure or uncertain in particular situations. Knowing children and their needs is therefore a key to the development of self-confident children who will be much more likely to know how to respond if confronted with a range of difficult situations or choices.

For children to be seen as strong and healthy, they need to be perceived as 'belonging' to the communities in which they grow up, where they can be encouraged to explore and relate to other members. Developing an understanding of the needs of the child should wherever possible be a shared one promoting joint constructions between parents, carers and practitioners, and the children themselves. In this context children will be more likely to develop as resilient because of the shared sense of community support in place. Children should attract a sense of shared responsibility in ensuring that they are safe from ill-treatment through the involvement of the child's own community of carers. The place of Children's Centres and other integrated and extended provision with clear aims to develop a set of preventative roles that encourage and support children and their carers is an important development in line with the Children Act 1989 (HMSO 1989) and the new

Children' Bill (House of Lords 2004) with their emphasis on working together in partnership with parents and carers. The child protection system is being developed so that cooperation between all professional practitioners and carers involved with children should also reduce the risk of ill-treatment through improved communication systems.

The case studies referred to provide interesting examples of proactive development work with parents and their very young children and illustrate possibilities for community support that are effective and positively perceived. The role of carers has been shown as central in the recognition and referral of abuse and the support of families and young children.

References

Beswick, J. and Pendrill, J. (2004) *The Feeding Service Annual Report*, January (unpublished).

Colton, M., Sanders, R. and Williams, M. (2001) *An Introduction to Working with Children: A Guide for Social Workers*. Basingstoke: Palgrave.

Culpitt, I. (1999) *Social Policy and Risk*. London: Sage.

David, T., Goouch, K., Powell, S. and Abbott, L. (2003) *Birth to Three Matters: A Review of the Literature (Research Report RR444)*. Nottingham: DfES Publications.

DfES (2002) *Birth to Three Matters*. London: DfES Publications.

DoH (2000) *The Framework for the Assessment of Children in Need and Their Families*. London: The Stationery Office.

DoH (2000) *Protecting Children, Supporting Parents: A Consultation Document on the Physical Punishment of Children*. London: DoH.

Douglas, M. (1986) *Risk Acceptability According to the Social Sciences*. London: Routledge and Kegan Paul.

Douglas, M. (1992) *Risk and Blame: Essays in Cultural Theory*. London: Routledge.

Gibbons, J., Gallagher, B., Bell, C. and Gordon, D. (1995) *Development After Physical Abuse in Early Childhood: Studies in Child Protection*. London: HMSO.

HMSO (1989) *Children Act 1989 (c.41)*. London: The Stationery Office.

HM Treasury (2003) *Every Child Matters*. London: The Stationery Office.

House of Lords (2004) *Children's Bill*. London: The Stationery Office.

Jackson, S. and Scott, S. (2000) Childhood, in G. Payne (ed.) *Social Divisions*. London: Macmillan Press.

James, A., Jenks, C. and Prout, A. (1998) *Theorising Childhood*. Cambridge: Polity Press, p. 38.

Lord Laming (2003) *The Victoria Climbié Inquiry, Report of an Inquiry*. Norwich: HMSO.

Marsh, A. (1994) People matter, in L. Abbott and R. Rodger (eds) *Quality Education in the Early Years*. Buckingham: Open University Press, p. 139.

Meggitt, C. (2001) *Baby and Child Health*. Oxford: Heinemann Educational Publishers.

Parton, N., Thorpe, D. and Wattam, C. (1997) *Child Protection: Risk and the Moral Order*. Basingstoke: Macmillan.

Powell, J. (1997) 'Who is listening?' – protecting young children from abuse, in L. Abbott and H. Moylett (eds) *Working with the Under-3s: Training and Professional Development*. Buckingham: Open University Press.

Raynor, P., Rudolph, M., Cooper, K., Marchant, P. and Cottrell, D. (1999) A randomised, controlled trial of specialist health visitor intervention for failure to thrive, *Archives of Disease in Childhood*, 80: 500–6.

Richardson, S. and Bacon, H. (eds) (2001) *Creative Responses to Child Sexual Abuse: Challenges and Dilemmas*. London and Philadelphia: Jessica Kingsley Publishers.

Skuse, D. (1993) Identification and management of problem eaters, *Archives of Disease in Childhood*, 69: 604–8.

Taylor, J. and Daniel, B. (1999) Interagency practice in children with non-organic failure to thrive: is there a gap between health and social care?, *Child Abuse Review*, 8: 325–38.

10 Observation Matters

Peter Elfer

Introduction

Peter Elfer is someone for whom close observation of children has long been central to his work as a parent, practitioner and trainer. From his work with Dorothy Selleck and Elinor Goldschmied to his contribution to the *Birth to Three Matters* project as a valued, supportive and sensitive Steering Group member, his abiding message has been that 'observation matters'. In this chapter he shares this belief with the next generation of early years practitioners.

Boring babies!

Are babies boring? You may feel shocked to read such a question, particularly in a book all about babies, toddlers and children under 3. Yet my own experience of talking to nursery staff is that many feel that work with the youngest children is often seen as the least challenging and skilled: 'it's all feeding and changing and they don't do much'. Why should there be this perception, when research studies of babies and toddlers reveal this period as one of intense growth and development and when close family members can be so excited about the tiny details of babies' looks, gestures and responses?

It is true that babies' care involves much that is routine and repetitious – early years practitioners, just as parents, can experience these aspects of care as boring. One understandable way for practitioners to minimize the risk of boredom is to keep busy. With a statutory staff to babies ratio of 1:3, keeping busy is not difficult! But in the 'busyness' of managing the day, how many details get lost? Is it all changing and feeding, getting up and settling to sleep?

Looking, listening and noting

On each of the 16 Component cards of the *Birth to Three Matters* Framework (DfES 2002) there is a box labelled, 'Look, listen, note'. Here the Framework invites practitioners to be aware of and alert to important things to look out for. For example, on the Emotional Well-being Component card, the box suggests:

Look, listen, note

- Observe and note the sounds and facial expressions young babies make in response to affectionate attention from their parent or their key person;
- Note verbal and non-verbal expressions of feelings...
- Observe sounds and facial expressions...
- Note examples of healthy independence...

These pointers are particularly helpful because they encourage practitioners to focus in on the fine details of children's body language or emotional expression.

Many practitioners working with babies and toddlers seem to be extremely good at this 'looking, listening and noting'. In the following quotations from practitioners speaking about babies' explorations, struggles and achievements, their voices are filled with pleasure and excitement.

We've got little Alice, Alice is quite new and she's sort of first she was really attached to Brigid now she comes and gives me a cuddle which is quite new because before she's not a very touchy feely baby, she likes her own little space and now she's started to come and she comes over and gives me a cuddle ... I think she's learning to trust us a bit.
(Teresa)

John ... he was in the sensory room with the bubble tube and he was making the noise going bub, bub, bub and then one day he went bubble and it was like oh that's amazing because we encouraged him to keep going with the initial sound and then he just managed to say it and then after that he can't stop.
(Brigid)

From their emotional tone as well as the words they actually use, it is almost as if the staff have been filled up with the feelings that the babies might have, feelings of excitement, confidence and achievement.

Yet when this 'looking, listening and noting' gets written down as an 'observation', it can also seem as if much of the detail and feeling can become lost. For example, in the following written observations of a 12-month-old (Alex) and an 18-month-old (Graham) what the staff have written does not seem to quite match the way they speak about the children.

> Alex has been exploring the shape sorter, he turned it round several times and put his hand through one of the shape holes.
>
> Graham has been exploring the bubble tube in the sensory room. Graham played with the balls and explored the plastic pots.
> (Elfer forthcoming)

Much of the emotional expression that was in the earlier voices and that told us something about the significance of what the baby or toddler had achieved seems to have gone in these brief observations. In short, these observations do not seem to do justice to what we know babies are capable of when we **hear** them described by a practitioner rather than when we **read about** them from written observations.

The authors of the framework have been clever in labelling this section of the Component cards 'Look, listen, note' rather than 'observation' or 'record keeping' or some other more 'professional' words. Perhaps they have recognized that what practitioners 'notice' about babies and toddlers is often so much more detailed and exciting than what actually gets recorded as an observation record.

What part do our emotional responses have to play in helping us observe? Much of what we convey to one another as human beings is not only through what we hear being told to us, or what we see from a person's body language, but what we feel. Human beings evoke feelings in one another as part of the whole repertoire of their communications. To show how true this is, think of how quickly we can tell, especially with people we know well, if they are sad, or preoccupied or excited about something, even before they have opened their mouths to speak to us. This is sometimes even more evident when we are with someone and feel that what they are telling us does not fit with our feelings about their communication. We may feel something is 'not quite right' or that we are having the wool pulled over our eyes. Our subjective feelings can seem to be a much better clue to the 'truth' than what we are more objectively hearing or seeing.

This is the case too with babies and young children, who are very powerful communicators of feeling. Everybody knows about the emotional power of a baby's cry and how someone who knows a baby very well can tell a lot from the feelings evoked in him or her by different kinds of cries.

To work well with babies and children under 3, it has been argued that a member of staff who is a 'key person' is needed for each child (Elfer et al. 2003). In addition to this organizational approach to providing consistency and intimacy in nurseries, perhaps we should also extend the methods of observation that we use to see the outcomes of these relationships in action.

Alongside conventional methods of observation in early years practice, where the emphasis is on recording selected behaviours and events, we now need to seek a method of observation that **does** allow us to record our feelings. This is **not** an alternative to tried and tested methods but an **additional** method to strengthen our efforts to observe holistically, to get into the baby's shoes, to try and see from their perspective, to be open to their feelings.

This has to be done immensely carefully because whilst the feelings that can be evoked in us by a baby may be a very good indication of how the baby is feeling, they may equally be more to do with the observer than the baby. We do want to get closer to understanding each baby's experience. But we do not want to get so close that we are muddling up our own feelings with those of the baby.

This chapter will describe such a method of observation that is focused on feelings as well as external behaviours. The method was 'tested' by a small group of experienced early years practitioners who tried out the observation method in a range of settings.

I hope that their findings will be a support and encouragement to other practitioners to consider using this method in addition to their own existing methods and procedures for observing babies.

Feelings as part of the picture

Professional practitioners struggle all the time to be as 'objective' as possible. Being objective matters because it is important to make our judgements and decisions concerning a child on the basis of evidence and not prejudice.

However, it is never possible to be completely objective: 'As human observers, it is inevitable that our own feelings and interpretations influence what we see or don't see' (Rolfe 2001: 231).

It is remarkable how people describe their first assessment of nurseries in terms of feelings. An experienced practitioner or inspector might commonly say that they can tell within a few minutes of stepping into a nursery whether this is somewhere they are likely to feel confident about the care of children or whether they get very early feelings of concern or anxiety.

With the help of another experienced person to think through and draw out these feelings and their origin, the practitioner may be able to piece together some of the tiny details of what it was that made them feel so positively or so negatively about the nursery. The origins of their feelings, when traced back, are likely to be based on some quite subtle details to do with the tone of voice of a member of staff, the manner of holding a baby or perhaps a baby's bodily response or facial expression reacting to how she or he is being held. These tiny but crucial details of what is **seen and heard** are usually also accompanied by **feelings** evoked in the observer by the particular interactions they are witnessing.

As these details are teased out, the feeling and evidence of why the practitioner felt positively or negatively might grow, and further details may come to be recalled. The person with whom they are talking might ask them to explain or think further about a particular movement or interaction. As this debriefing or 'talking out' continues, the initial assessment may be confirmed, or alternatively, the whole picture might begin to change as it is recalled and examined.

A method of observation particularly designed to enable us to think about our affective response (that is, the feelings evoked in us) as well as our sensory response (what we see and hear) has been developed at the Tavistock Clinic Foundation, now part of the Camden and North Islington NHS Trust in London.

The Tavistock Method

The Tavistock Method of infant or young child observation has been described on a video called *Observation Observed* (Miller 2002) with an accompanying outline of the nature and practice of observation by Miller. At the heart of this method of observation lies the fact that we are able not only to **see and hear** the reactions and responses of another person but also have the capacity to have feelings evoked in us by another person. The main features of the observation method, as it applies to observations of babies in the home over a long (two-year) period have been described by Michael Rustin (1989).

Miller adds in the booklet that accompanies the video *Observation Observed* (2002) that:

> Perhaps it seems surprising that parents should agree to a stranger entering their family at such a vulnerable time of change and growth. However, they are often pleased to find someone as interested in baby as they are themselves, and as the visits continue their regular pattern each family makes its own individual relationship with their observer.
>
> (Miller 2002: 2)

So it seems that observing and noticing, depending on how it is managed, can feel both intrusive and exposing in a negative way or affirming and developmental in a more positive way.

Infant observation with children under 3 in nursery

In order for the method to be adapted for use in early years childcare and education, some key changes need to be made. For example, and perhaps most importantly, it would be impossible for most practitioners to observe the same child once a week for two years, as the method recommends! Most nurseries could not afford to release a practitioner to observe for a whole hour once each week. The relationship between the observer and the child is different too. Observing in the home, from the time the baby is born, allows the observer to establish a particular kind of relationship with the baby and family. This relationship is not one where the observer sometimes switches to being a carer, looking after the baby, and it is not one where the observer becomes a friend of the family although their interactions together will of course be 'friendly'.

This is very different in the nursery where the observer definitely is also a carer for the children and where the observer and carers will also be colleagues and perhaps friends too. However, a crucial factor that is common to both the Tavistock Method of observation and the use of this approach to observation in early years settings, is the preparation of a written record as soon as possible after the observations have taken place.

This written record can then be shared with supervisors and colleagues so that it can be thought about and discussed. This part of the observation process is essential to support the person who has done the observations and to help this person examine and explore the differing possible meanings of the observation for the baby's experience.

The key features of infant observation in an early years setting can be summarized as follows:

Infant observation in the nursery

- An early years practitioner observes for between 10 and 20 minutes, focusing on one child and her or his interactions with adults, other children and with toys and objects.
- The practitioner observes without notebook, concentrating as far as possible on the chosen child, and being as receptive as possible to the smallest of details as well as emotional atmosphere and responses.
- After the observation, the practitioner makes a written record of the observation, writing in as free-flowing a way as possible, following the main sequence of events and recording details as they come back to mind.
- The written observations are shared with supervisor / colleagues and discussed, differing interpretations and connections being considered and examined.
- The practitioner continues to observe, bringing further write-ups to the group to be discussed and compared.

Dorothy Selleck and I have previously described observing in this way with children under 3 in nurseries (Elfer and Selleck 1999). However, we did so from the point of view of researchers. What would a group of practitioners think about using this method of observation? How would they experience sitting, without notebook, and trying to be as open-minded and emotionally receptive as possible? Would they regard the method as a useful additional tool in developing practice with babies and children under 3?

In order to begin to address these questions, a group of eight students studying for the MA in Early Childhood Studies at the University of Surrey Roehampton undertook to use the method. Of the group, seven were qualified in nursery nursing or teaching and were experienced in direct or advisory work with babies and children under 3. They were asked to describe their experience of observing in this way and to evaluate how much they felt this method of observation helped them see from the baby's point of view.

Observation observed

The students each observed between one and four babies or toddlers, aged from 6½ months to 27 months, once a week for between four and eight weeks. These were babies and toddlers known to the students either through personal contacts, for example through family or friendship networks, or through professional contacts, for example children in nurseries where the student was a member of staff or had a visiting advisory role. In the training of child psychotherapists, students are advised to arrange to observe a baby from a family with whom they have little or no prior relationship. This enables the student to establish the observation role without it being influenced by another relationship (friendship or professional responsibility) between the observer and the child and family. In this sense, the absence of a relationship between the observer and the baby and family prior to observation commencing is helpful. However, in the much shorter term observations that the students were being asked to undertake, and in the context of early years practitioners testing out this method of observation, students often did have a professional and/or personal relationship with the family as well as an 'observer – observed' relationship.

The observations each lasted for between ten minutes and one hour. The observations were typed up, usually one or two pages long at most, and we met together each week, focusing on one observation at a time and supporting one another to question and clarify possible meanings and understandings.

Only one of the students started the observations with an interest or focus on a particular aspect of how the babies and adults interacted together. This student aimed to:

Focus on the opportunities for celebrating the experiences of the babies and infants in a toddler and carer group. These did not have to be achievements; they could be discoveries, attempts that succeeded and those that failed. They could be social experiences and personal ones, emotional and creative, and I was particularly interested in how children's independence was encouraged and celebrated...

(Judith)

As one possible focus, this is important, because it links directly with the Emotional Well-being Component of the Aspect A Healthy Child (DfES 2002). Yet this Component rightly emphasizes the importance of promoting healthy *dependence* as well as independence in supporting emotional well-being. Observing interactions that support both *dependence* and *independence* in babies and young children involves much reliance on the observer's feelings about how an adult responds and how a baby or toddler copes with this response. For adults to get this 'right' involves subtle and finely tuned responses, and knowing whether the adult has got this more or less 'right' or not is usually revealed in the fine details of how the child reacts. Could this method of observation help to highlight these fine details?

What about the experience of the other students? Reading their stories of their experience, there are some strikingly common themes:

- the power of this method of close observation – being allowed to record feelings and the freedom from having to make notes allows you to see a lot;
- observing so closely has a powerful emotional impact on the observer;
- observing in this way raises particular ethical issues.

The power of close observation

Not having to make any kind of written record during the observations seemed to be experienced by these observers as enabling them to come closer to the child's experience. Judith talked about a sense of 'The total immersion of the observer in the child and their environment with the opportunity to open up to the deep personal emotions aroused during the observations'.

Perhaps this is what Gunilla Dahlberg and her colleagues were referring to when they describe **swimming** in observations (Dahlberg, Moss and Pence 1999). Rebecca seemed to have a similar experience, 'I was so engrossed in this observation and amazed at how much detail I remembered'.

The detailed descriptions that resulted from these very close observations did indeed seem to have great value as material for a team of early years workers to discuss and think about. For example, Judith observes:

> Watching Miriam's focused care of her children, she encouraged them to be independent and celebrated their efforts, I wondered how it would be possible to support other carers to reach that level of awareness of the needs of the children. It appeared to me that the children in Miriam's care had a very strong self concept...

However, she adds, 'I felt that there was a general desire to support and encourage children but that this desire was sometimes misdirected. Often a general "good girl" or "lovely" would be thrown into the air without anyone knowing to what it referred.'

The closeness of Meryl's observation leads her to think perhaps the staff working with Tom, aged 12 months, have misunderstood his response:

> Tom now explores this (the activity centre fixed to a gate) with great interest and is joined by a staff member. This is more, I feel, due to the fact that he is positioned in a doorway, a potentially dangerous area. She interacts with him momentarily before lifting him back to the centre of the toddler area where she leaves him. Tom immediately cries in protest I feel, at being physically moved without his knowledge or agreement. The staff present however interpret this as Tom being tired.

Anne too uses her close observation to question the response of staff:

> Child 'A' (a boy of 7 months) is sitting on a soft rug with the adult and is handed a plastic rattle which he puts in his mouth. The adult takes it away saying 'No' and gives him a teething ring. As he goes to put this in his mouth, this too is removed and he is given a plastic toy with buttons to press. Why he was not allowed to mouth toys or to have his actions commented on may be a remnant of too much emphasis on hygiene ... throughout, his facial expressions remained the same, that of detachment, as though he has already learned not to be too curious about things as they are constantly removed.

Lastly, Siobhan, observing in a home setting, speaks of Matilda's (aged 6½ months) thinking:

> Overall, I had the impression of a mind engaging constantly and deeply in experience upon experience. It is a time of rapid discovery for child and parent alike. In observation two, Matilda's play with her

new cup is a source of fascination for both, 'she puts the spout in her mouth and chews against the rubber. It makes an interesting squeaky sound. She seems completely absorbed in the actions and the listening, and moves it around in her mouth using her tongue and her hands ... her mother sits down on a chair at the table nearby and watches her, 'she's never done this before!' she says to me.

The possibilities raised by these three observers are of course only that – 'possibilities'. More observations and discussion with other workers in the same setting would be needed to begin to confirm them or to change them. The point is that the degree of detail and the record of the observers' feelings seems to be enabling possibilities to be discussed that would otherwise perhaps not even have been considered.

The emotional impact of close observations

The observations seemed also to have the effect of bringing the observer and the child observed emotionally close. Some of the observers described how they felt a growing sense of connection with the child they were observing:

> The total immersion of the observer in the child and her/his environment with the opportunity to open up to the deep personal emotions aroused during the observations, to 'swim in observations' helps them develop their ability to focus, remember and relate.
>
> (Judith)

> Tom 'got used to me' but is this right? His recognition of me appeared from week two, and we built a relationship that was from my point of view surprisingly warm and familiar. I even referred to him as 'mine' and felt an emotional bond with him.
>
> (Meryl)

> It is significant that the observation lasted for an extra five minutes due perhaps to the observer's immersion in Jake's concentration, reflecting the extent to which the child's 'self' was not only seen but also experienced.
>
> (Heidi)

> I was so engrossed in this observation and amazed at how much detail I remembered.
>
> (Rebecca)

Yet whilst this closeness could be fascinating for the observer, their accounts made it plain that it could also be anxiety-provoking in Naoko's case and uncomfortable in a different way for Rebecca:

...she lifted Mia and stood up. She rocked Mia as if she was dancing in the air! Her legs swung right to left. She shouted excitedly. I was surprised because her mother shook Mia roughly. However, Mia guffawed at this play! Mia was lifted as high as an adult's height and swung roughly. It was possible that Mia might cry. However, she did not seem to be scared and she did not scream, on the contrary, she looked happy with this play. It seems that she believed that her mother would not hurt her, so she could enjoy this play. There might be joy of play with her mother. However, I was scared by this play.

(Naoko)

However difficult the situation, it is important to hold onto your own feelings as a way of trying to think about the evidence, even if they are feelings of discomfort. How do you observe the things you don't want to see...

(Rebecca)

As these two observers note, close observations will sometimes involve seeing things we do not want to see and how do we cope with that? One answer to this is the critical role of supervisors and colleagues. Their job is to provide support through listening to what the experience has been like for the observer and to help the observer think about different possible meanings of the observation beyond the first ideas of the observer (first thoughts and ideas may often need refining or possibly changing completely).

Ethics matter

Finding a way to hear and think about the voice of the child (for babies expressed through the power of their emotional communications) is part of our legal responsibility towards children (Children Act 1989; Convention on the Rights of the Child, UN 1989). We also have a commitment to exercise this responsibility in an ethical way. The observers using this method of observation were alert to this:

I also experienced feelings of discomfort when I realized that the child I was watching was also observing me ... this experience heightened my awareness that I was in a way invading these children's privacy.

(Anne)

I hated this experience. I felt that I was interrupting and intruding into what seemed a very intimate exchange. It felt totally unnatural not to talk and join in when Tom looked at me which he did continually.

(Meryl)

Observing so closely perhaps will sometimes feel as if it is observing **too** closely, that we are seeing right inside the child. Is seeing too much as bad as not seeing enough? Maybe the answer to this depends on the reasons for our 'seeing'. Are we observing to be voyeuristic, or intrusive, or are we observing in order to understand and use this understanding to help match our planning and responses to babies and very young children more effectively?

Observation can be double-edged and how it is undertaken, or not, the way we manage our encounters with the youngest children, is precisely what has been described as the 'ethics of an encounter' (Dahlberg et al. 1999: 106). The way we respond in our encounters with children, for example how much time we give to observing, what we are prepared to see or what we can tolerate to notice, are all part of our subjective responses. One way of thinking about the ethics of our encounters with children is to think about these subjective responses.

As John illustrates from his experience, we can take some account of our subjectivity by thinking about three different ways this method of observation might put us particularly at risk of distorting our understanding of the child's experience:

- The observer's close emotional presence in the observation – what the observer sees is not a true account of what would have happened had the observer not been there ... but ... the observer needs to be not only in the Unit but part of it as it is only experiences of the minute by minute dynamics of interactions that yield the nuances and subtleties of human behaviour; CCTV would not yield the same degree of involvement.
- Because there is no recording of events at the time, the observer might subconsciously construct events that did not happen because this would fit in with the observer's subjective feelings about what was happening ... however as the object of the exercise is actually to gain information on subjective feelings and emotional states this may not necessarily be a significant problem.
- Where there are class and race differences between the observer and the observed, how can we be sure that there are not cultural or social influences on the subjective interpretations?

These are of course valid concerns, although certainly not exclusive to this method of observation. They serve to remind us of the importance of the scrutiny of the observations with a supervisor or with colleagues, in order to

unpick ways in which the observations may have been presented or interpreted to fit the observer's feelings or particularly influenced by the observer's
social and ethnic background.

The students found 'thinking space' in which both feelings engendered
by the observation process itself, as well as the content of the observations,
could be discussed. For example, it seemed a relief to students to discover they
were not alone, when noticing quite intimate details of babies' interactions,
in experiencing a sense of intrusiveness.

Conclusion

What can be drawn from the experiences of these students as they used this
method of observation, first in individual encounters with babies and children under 3, and later in discussion in the seminar group? The students' own
conclusions are powerful:

> This intense method of observation, combined with the necessary
> training offers a remarkable tool with which infants and practitioners
> can grow and develop. It is a lens through which emotions are ex-
> posed, explored and valued as significant contributors to an evolving
> and dynamic set of relationships.
>
> (Heidi)

> This kind of observation offers an important and powerful way of
> accessing data about human interactions that moves away from
> considering solely the cognitive explanations of how humans in-
> teract.
>
> (John)

However, we must be cautious. This group is small and only one group.
Alongside their very positive assessment of the value of this method of observation, they have identified many issues about how the method is carried
out. Maybe readers, committed to realizing the aims of the *Birth to Three
Matters* Framework (DfES 2002), in particular to:

- value and celebrate babies and children;
- provide opportunities for reflection on practice;
- acknowledge that working with babies and children is complex,
  challenging and demanding

will now extend the experience of the student group and explore this method of observation for themselves.

Acknowledgements

I would like to acknowledge and warmly thank the students whose observations and evaluations provide the core material for this chapter.

References

Dahlberg, G., Moss, P. and Pence, A. (1999) *Beyond Quality in Early Childhood Education and Care. Postmodern Perspectives*. London: Falmer Press.

DfES (2002) *Birth to Three Matters*. London: DfES Publications.

Elfer, P. (forthcoming) Ph.D thesis, *Organising for intimacy in the care of babies and children under three attending full time nursery*. University of East London.

Elfer, P., Goldschmied, E. and Selleck, D. (2003) *Key Persons in the Nursery: Building Relationships for Quality Provision*. London: David Fulton Publishers.

Elfer, P. and Selleck, D. (1999) Children under three in nurseries. Uncertainty as a creative factor in child observations, *European Early Childhood Research Journal*, Vol.7 (1).

HMSO (1989) *Children Act 1989*. London: The Stationery Office.

Miller, L. (1989) Introduction, in L. Miller, M. Rustin and J. Shuttleworth (eds) *Closely Observed Infants*. London: Duckworth.

Miller, L. (2002) *Observation Observed: An Outline of the Nature and Practice of Infant Observation (Videos and Booklet)*. London: The Tavistock Clinic Foundation.

Rolfe, S. (2001) Direct observation, in G. MacNaughton, S. Rolfe and I. Siraj-Blatchford (eds) *Doing Early Childhood Research: International Perspectives on Theory and Practice*. Buckingham: Open University Press.

Rustin, M. (1989) Observing infants: reflections on methods, in L. Miller, M. Rustin and J. Shuttleworth (eds) *Closely Observed Infants*. London: Duckworth.

United Nations (1989) *Convention on the Rights of the Child*. http://www.unicef.org/crc/crc.htm

11 Play Matters

Tina Bruce

Introduction

Anyone who knows Tina or has read any of her impressive range of publications will know that for her play really does matter. From her earliest writing to her most recent book, her commitment to a child's right to play unrestricted or confined by adult rules and expectations is a central precept. Tina is a true Froebelian. Her Twelve Features of Free-Flow Play (Bruce 1991) are known worldwide and continue to influence practitioners in their work across countries, communities and settings. Tina played a valuable role as a member of the Steering and Working Groups for the *Birth to Three Matters* project. In this chapter, in which she challenges us to consider why play matters, her own commitment is self-evident.

Play is a birth to death process

So often in life the things that matter most are the most difficult to understand. Play is just such a process. Its workings are often hidden, subtle and sophisticated in the way it impacts on development and learning. The results of early childhood play are often hard to causally relate and link with later achievements. We are only at the beginning of understanding why play is an important learning mechanism, and how it develops to give children the possibility to apply, consolidate and try out different aspects of learning in their lives.

The way that play contributes to the development of creative, flexible thinking; the possibility to face pain, cope and deal with it by gaining the control that brings resilience; helps the processes involved in reflecting, rearranging, imagining, making alternatives; provides connections with past and future; and takes us out of the constraints of the immediate, are as yet little understood. The more we delve into the inner workings of play, the more we shall gain in helping not just children but also adults to develop and learn throughout their lives.

This is because play is a birth to death process. It is an integrating mechanism. This means that it helps people, at any stage of their lives, to consolidate, coordinate and get together what they know, feel and understand in ways which give them a sense of control over what is happening to them. Those who feel that life does things to them in unstoppable ways develop low self-esteem, and poor self-identity. They become reactive, disempowered babies, toddlers, young children, children in middle childhood, and then teenagers and adults. Play helps people to be proactive and dynamic, autonomous learners, and to step out of passivity in their learning at any point in life.

The beginnings of play (Forbes 2004) are already present in babies, toddlers and young children. In this chapter the focus will be on this period of life, using the *Birth to Three Matters* (DfES 2002) document as a Framework. However, it is important to bear in mind that these are only the beginnings, hopefully, of a lifetime through which play will make a rich contribution.

Which comes first? The Birth to Three Matters Framework supports children's developing play – but play supports the Framework

It is difficult, if not impossible, to argue which comes first. Because play is a learning mechanism (Bruce 1991) which can be seen also as an organizing principle (Brown 1998), it makes the learning holistic by bringing what is known and understood together.

During the first three years, play supports children. It helps them in becoming healthy, developing well-being, growing and developing, finding out about safety and in making healthy choices as part of living and learning. Play helps children from birth to 3 to be strong, to know themselves, in all dimensions as Me, Myself and I, as they are acknowledged and affirmed by others. In this way they become self-assured and develop a sense of belonging which will continue to be important until death. The *Birth to Three Matters* Framework (DfES 2002) can in fact be a framework for learning throughout life. Play is part of becoming a skilful communicator, finding a voice, being 'together' with others, listening and responding to people, and making sense of it all. Play helps us to be competent learners who can make connections, be imaginative, creative and able to represent our experiences.

Observing play and acting on our observations to further support it

Because play is important throughout our lives, we need to establish and refine ways of observing it and helping it along, which are appropriate for every point in life, and for diverse lives. In 1991, a trawl of the theoretical and research literature on play in the English language, or translated into English, revealed recurrent themes which suggested that some order could be placed on the unwieldy word 'play'. This helped in addressing the fact that play was a term used with different meanings by different people, as an umbrella word under which all sorts of things were placed.

Games and recreation were often conflated with play, rather than seen as distinct but related to it. However, beneath the seeming chaos of descriptions and diverse theories on the subject, there lurked areas of 'common' usage, or different usage, which when identified led to reflection, bringing the kinds of debate and discussion likely to facilitate the development of reflective practice in relation to play. This exploration developed into twelve features of play, under the heading 'free-flow play' (Bruce 1991, 1996b, 2001, 2002).

Twelve features of play

1. In their play, children use the first-hand experiences that they have in life.
2. Children make up rules as they play, and so keep control of their play.
3. Children symbolically represent as they play, making play props.
4. Children choose to play. They cannot be made to play.
5. Children rehearse possible futures in their role play.
6. Children pretend when they play.
7. Children sometimes play alone.
8. Children and/or adults play together, as companions, or cooperatively in pairs or groups.
9. Each player has a personal play agenda, although they may not be aware of this.
10. Children playing will be deeply involved and difficult to distract from their deep learning. Children at play wallow in their learning.
11. Children try out their most recent learning, skills and competencies when they play. They seem to celebrate what they know.
12. Children at play coordinate their ideas, feelings and make sense of relationships with their family, friends and culture. When play is coordinated it flows along in a sustained way. It is called free-flow play.

(developed from Bruce 1991)

In this chapter, we shall look at some examples of babies, toddlers and young children involved in free-flow play. Further reference to free-flow play can be found on the CD-ROM from the *Birth to Three Matters* Framework (2002). Free-flow play is also referred to in the training video for the *Foundation Stage Profile* (DfES/QCA 2003) to aid assessment and support learning in the reception year. The twelve features of free-flow play can be used as a tool for observing and reflecting on play at any stage of life, embracing diversity and inclusion across age, gender, culture, disability, special educational needs, or economic background. Anyone can play. Not all do. It is now seen as a human right for children to play (United Nations 1989). This is not so for adults – yet.

Getting in the mood for play

In this chapter, because of the remit of this book, the focus will necessarily be on getting the play off to a good start during the first three years. This involves getting in the mood for play. Babies sometimes signal to us that they are in the mood to play, and sometimes adults 'suggest' the moment is right. We do this by exaggerated gestures, sounds and pauses, and facial expressions (Trevarthen 1998). The flow of play can go in a very light-hearted direction, which is signalled on both sides by playfulness (Garvey 1977). This takes everyone involved from real-life behaviour (literal behaviour) into play mode (non-real and non-literal behaviour). On the video which is part of the *Birth to Three Matters* Framework (DfES 2002) materials package, we see a childminder and the two children she cares for moving into play, through their shared pleasure, in action and rhythm, of the 'tickle tickle' part of the story book they are sharing together. The toddler takes part first, and the baby rapidly joins the fun. Most people emphasize the enjoyment of play when discussing its importance. However, this is only one part of the contribution play makes to development and learning.

Children and adults also signal to us in other ways that they are in the mood to play. The baby who is playing with the red and blue ball in the same video (DfES 2002) is very serious as he plays. This links with the view of play held by Froebel, that play is the highest and most serious form of learning, because it helps children to make sense of their lives, the ideas, feelings and relationships they are coming to know about and understand, and the way their learning is embodied in their physical selves (Liebschner 1992).

Both the group play between the childminder and children and the sitting baby's play are examples of free-flow play, but for different reasons and with different nuances, styles and personalities, cultural dimensions, contexts and many other facets during the two different play scenarios. The first play scenario develops from playful beginnings, and the second from deep engagement with a ball in companionship with a supportive adult and another baby (Piaget 1952). Offering sitting babies interesting objects so that they can make choices is of central importance in developing play (Abbott and Moylett 1997; Manning-Morton and Thorpe 2003), so are helpful adults, who are sensitive observers, offering support without dominating or taking over the play (Forbes 2004).

From an early age, babies can turn-take, and the 'peek-a-boo' tradition

(Bruner 1996) or, in this case, the joyous anticipation of being tickled, are early aspects of games which contribute to the twelve features of free-flow play. Previous experience of the pleasure of this kind of game supports the swift move into play. Games are powerful in this, because they offer security through predictability of the rules. The playfulness that often accompanies these simple games opens up everyone involved to the possibility of entering the depth of free-flow play, with its need for courage, risk-taking and embracing the unknown.

Reflecting on the play

So far we have found the first two features of play to be present in this play scenario. Everyone is using previous knowledge of the rules of 'tickle' games. First-hand experience and use of the game's rules are present here. They are also using the third feature because they are using each other as play props. The tummy is tickled, or the baby touches the adult's face. No one told them to do this. The play scenario emerged spontaneously. Everyone had a choice about whether or not to join the 'tickle' game. It involves all three. This is a delightful video sequence, and of great value to the development and learning of the children. However, there is no rehearsal for the future, or pretending. It does not involve a personal play agenda for anyone. This is a well-known, time-honoured, cross-cultural, traditional game, with well-established rules. It is great fun, and it seems to develop into a deeper plunge into free-flow play, in which learning is demonstrated by being applied in earnest with the all-consuming energy that is part of learning through play. This is because it integrates the feelings, ideas and relationships with the physical aspects of, in this case, becoming a bookworm.

The three features missing (5, 6 and 7 from the list in the box) involve entering other worlds, rehearsal and roles (feature 5), pretending (feature 6), and no one is alone in this play scenario (feature 7). This is joint, social play. The toddler may well in other situations become involved in free-flow play which includes entering other roles, pretending and symbolic behaviour. She may also, on occasions, choose to play alone. The baby has yet to develop the symbolic side of play.

The twelve features help us to look at play as it flows, without having to pin it down. The same child might play in different ways, drawing on different features, in different situations and contexts, or with different people. It seems that unless play flows, it goes. We need to observe play so that we plot its flow, which will have changing nuances and emphases from moment to moment. Having seen the rich free-flow play of the book sharing together, we are left wondering how the play will flow next for this baby, toddler and childminder.

Linking the observation of play with the *Birth to Three Matters* Framework

The twelve features of free-flow play are helping the baby and toddler to be strong, healthy children, who are competent learners and skilful communicators.

The tickling aids the children in developing a sense of embodiment, which is (Davies 2003; Trevarthen 2004) a crucial part of knowing themselves: Me, Myself and I. The children are each acknowledged and affirmed by the adult, both physically through the play and in the way the baby is cuddled and snuggles in, and also through the ideas, feelings and relationships. When the toddler speaks, the adult listens carefully and accepts, often expanding what is said. We can see the baby's contribution taken up too. This brings a sense of belonging, and self-assurance develops. Playing together in sharing a book has been a powerful means of developing the Aspect, A Strong Child from the *Birth to Three Matters* Framework (DfES 2002). An analysis of all the Aspects would have a similar result.

Feeling safe enough to dare to play

In the *Birth to Three Matters* (DfES 2002) video, Nicky, who is with a group of children, is teaching them an action song. Action songs are musical games, as opposed to mathematical (such as dominoes) or social games (for example, please and thank-you, greetings and partings, waving goodbye). Games of all kinds will feed into the twelve features of play, developing self-assurance in individual children so that they can access free-flow play.

The unpredictability of what might happen in free-flow play can be a challenge for some children, especially those with complex needs and special educational needs. Toddlers easily feel unsafe when they don't know what is happening as they participate socially. The clear rules of songs and dances (such as 'Round and Round the Garden, like a Teddy Bear', or 'Ring a Ring a Roses') help children to predict and anticipate, which gives a feeling of control. Children feel safe, and begin to make choices, when their emotional well-being is nurtured. These are important Components in the Aspect of the *Birth to Three Matters* Framework (DfES 2002) A Healthy Child.

Changing rules, and adapting them for your own purposes, means that children have to know the rules. It takes courage requiring self-assurance and emotional well-being (two Components of A Strong Child and A Healthy Child respectively) to see what happens when the rules are rearranged, not knowing what might happen or where the free-flowing play might lead. Knowing you can escape by leaving the play, or gain control by inserting your own self-made rules into it, gives children access to increasing flexibility in thinking, and adaptive behaviour. This helps ideas, thoughts, feelings and relationships to be applied during play in ways which make a child strong, healthy, a competent learner and a skilled communicator.

Very young children need to know a song, dance, story, or social rule exceptionally well before they can play with changing it. They may not be able to tolerate adaptations to it. This is because the symbolic behaviour of role play and images, and the world of pretend are only just opening up to become part of their play. The other features of play are present earlier.

We use what we know and can do when we play

Returning to the play scenario of the sitting baby, seriously contemplating the red and blue ball, we gain a different perspective of free-flowing play. He is so young that he does not have much experience of the properties of a ball, but he uses what he knows. The balls can be picked up, dropped and banged, on things and people. Gopnik et al. (1999) emphasize that we use what we know to explore what we don't know, and we need other people to help us. The baby is making his own rules as he plays, banging the ball on people and objects and surfaces. The red and blue ball, and the other baby and the adult's hand have been made into his play props. He chooses to do this, and has complete control over his decision whether or not to engage in this free-flow play episode.

He is playing alone, but there are indications of companionship from the adult and the other baby. He is deeply involved, and difficult to distract, wallowing in what he is doing. He is using his learning, and although there is some new learning, this is typical of free-flow play in that he is mainly using what he already knows, that you can bang objects together. He is experiencing banging two identical objects, the blue and red ball, on his friend's back, or the hand of the adult. The banging is an old behaviour, often described as a schema, which is a learning mechanism, Mandler (1999) suggests it also helps him to develop understanding about spatial and temporal relationships. During this play scenario, he is integrating his understanding of how spheres (in this case the red and blue balls) can be used, and how they can be banged on objects, surfaces and people. Banging is typical of babies who are sitting.

Once again the missing features of free-flow play are those relating to symbolic behaviour. Most children begin to develop this aspect of their free-flow play during the second year of life, but children with complex needs and learning difficulties are frequently challenged in this respect. Nevertheless, they can play in ways which are rich and helpful to their further learning.

We need to begin where the learner is in giving every child their right to play

Dave, who is 18 months old, cannot sit unaided, and perhaps never will. He has a visual and hearing impairment. He is lying on his back, but the adult has put some hanging objects around him. He seems to be looking at one placed near the top of his head to his right. He swipes in the air with his right arm. The adult moves the object so that as he swipes he hits the object with his hand. He smiles. Important features of play are present here. He knows from past experience that objects can be looked at, reached for and touched. He needed help to bring this about (Nielsen 1992). He enjoys play props, and playing alone with the necessary help being provided. He is then able to pursue his personal play agenda. He is deeply engaged in his play, and he is using what he knows to the full. The free-flow play helps him to integrate his understanding of how objects behave, and how people relate to him.

So far, none of the examples discussed have included symbolic aspects of play. In the *Birth to Three Matters* (DfES 2002) video, however, there is a play scenario with children in the home corner which has been set up outside. A girl pretends to telephone her Daddy. She uses props which are near to reality. It is not clear whether she is 'herself' phoning him, or pretending to be someone else doing so. Neither is it clear whether she is being like someone phoning her Daddy, or pretending to be herself phoning her Daddy (Vygotsky 1978). This is typical of the pretend play of toddlers. Assuming another role in play is a huge step in development. She is imitating the actions of making a telephone call. She says her Daddy is not there, but toddlers often seem to half expect a voice to be at the other end when they appear to be pretending. It is as if the line between literal, real life and non-literal pretend, imaginative and representational symbol use is not yet clear for them. Even so, it is an amazing achievement to have got this far in not much more than a year of living. The human brain is an amazing organ, capable of constant and life-long development.

Becoming a symbol user

Becoming a symbol user is an important part of human development. A symbol is something which stands for something else. Adults can be very helpful in facilitating the development of role play and the world of pretend which opens up alternative, possible and impossible worlds by stating 'I'm pretending' when they join the role play, or pretend play scenario. Earlier in the chapter, the importance of playful signalling was emphasized as marking the move from literal to non-literal, and the entry into play. As discussed, the adult will make exaggerated movements, gestures and facial expressions and sounds, and the baby will respond, often giggling in anticipation. Similarly rough and tumble play is often heralded when one child or adult makes a huge gesture which in effect 'announces' the change from real life to play – chasing and catching. In the case of the food preparation play, so typical of toddlers, children are helped into symbolic play by the adult putting the change of mode into words, 'I'm pretending to eat my lunch', and then moving into the character and indulging in pretend eating. Gradually, as their spoken or signed language develops, children make these kinds of verbal 'announcement' quite spontaneously (Bateson 1955).

Play matters

We have seen in this chapter that play matters. It makes an important contribution to the way that children grow, develop and learn. The twelve features of free-flow play give a birth to death means of observing and cultivating play, which can be linked with the *Birth to Three Matters* Framework (DfES 2002). Just as we shall not find every feature of play present in every play scenario, so we shall not find every Aspect or Component to be there either. Different moments and episodes of play use the features of free-flow play and the Aspects and Components resonate with them according to the people and contextual situations in which the play arises. It is best not to pin children down as they begin to free-flow play, and so it is important to use methods of observing and cultivating play that embrace the Aspects which make strong, healthy children who are skilful communicators, and competent learners. Play is for life, but children whose play flows from birth onwards are going to take the Aspects and Components with them, using their childhood as a lifelong resource, rather than something they grow out of and lose.

References

Abbott, L. and Moylett, H. (1997) *Working with the Under Threes: Responding to Children's Needs*. Maidenhead: Open University Press.

Bateson, G. (1955) A theory of play and fantasy, *Psychiatric Research Reports*, 2: 39–51.

Brown, S. (1998) Play as an organising principle: clinical evidence and personal observations, in M. Bekoff and J. Byers (eds) *Animal Play: Evolutionary, Comparative and Ecological Perspectives*. Cambridge: Cambridge University Press.

Bruce, T. (1991) *Time to Play in Early Childhood Education*. London: Hodder and Stoughton.

Bruce, T. (1996) *Helping Young Children to Play*. London: Hodder and Stoughton.

Bruce, T. (2001) *Learning Through Play: Babies, Toddlers and the Foundation Years.* London: Hodder and Stoughton.

Bruce, T. and Meggitt, C. (2002) *Childcare and Education,* 3rd edn. London: Hodder and Stoughton.

Bruner, J. (1996) *The Culture of Education.* Cambridge, MA: Harvard University Press.

Davies, M. (2003) *Movement and Dance in Early Childhood,* 2nd edn. London: Paul Chapman Publishing.

DfES (2002) *Birth to Three Matters.* London: DfES Publications.

DfES/QCA (2003) *Foundation Stage Profile.* Suffolk: QCA Publications.

Dunn, J. (1998) *The Beginnings of Social Understanding.* Oxford: Blackwell.

Forbes, R. (2004) *Beginning to Play: Birth to Three.* Maidenhead: Open University Press.

Garvey, C. (1977) *Play.* London: Fontana/Open Books.

Gopnik, A., Meltzoff, A. and Kuhl, P. (1999) *How Babies Think.* London: Weidenfeld and Nicolson.

Liebschner, J. (1992) *A Child's Work: Freedom and Guidance in Froebel's Educational Theory and Practice.* Cambridge: Lutterworth Press.

Mandler, J. (1999) Pre-verbal representations and language, in P. Bloom, M. Peterson, L. Nadel and M. Garrett (eds) *Language and Space.* Cambridge, MA: MIT Press.

Manning-Morton, J. and Thorp, M. (2003) *Keytimes for Play: The First Three Years.* Maidenhead: Open University Press.

Nielsen, L. (1992) *Space and Self: Active Learning in the Little Room.* Copenhagen, Denmark: Sikon (available RNIB).

Piaget, J. (1952) *Play, Dreams and Imitation,* trans. C. Gattegno and F. Hodgson. London: Routledge and Kegan Paul.

Trevarthen, C. (1998) The child's need to learn a culture, in M. Woodhead, D. Faulkner and K. Littleton (eds) *Cultural Worlds of Early Childhood.* London: Routledge, in association with Open University Press.

Trevarthen, C. (2004) Foreword, in T. Bruce (ed.) *Developing Learning in Early Childhood.* London: Paul Chapman Publishing.

United Nations (1989) *Convention on the Rights of the Child.* http://www.unicef.org/crc/crc.htm

Vygotsky, L. (1978) *Mind in Society.* London: Harvard University Press.

12 Interaction Matters

Iram Siraj-Blatchford

Introduction

Iram Siraj-Blatchford has a passionate interest in young children and their learning as well as research and equality issues. The important messages in her chapter point to the inextricable links between thought and language and remind us that interaction is the basis for social as well as cognitive development. For this reason she was the ideal person to invite to write this authoritative chapter on why interaction matters for young children.

Background

In the early years, interaction with adults and other children is the key to acquisition of language. For infants and toddlers, their early interactions with parents and caregivers provide the basis for communication and learning in both the first or home language and in second language acquisition. These early infant–caregiver interactions establish a basis for communication and continue to be the context for the development of the child's language throughout the early years (Trevarthen 1992).

In the early months, babies smile and respond to sounds made by familiar people and react to familiar situations. According to Trevarthen (1992) babies actually initiate interaction and response from others, especially their parents. Between 6 and 12 months, babies observe and imitate others, are possessive about their own toys, babble and begin to make sounds. From 1 to 2 years, toddlers are becoming aware of their feelings, enjoy solitary and parallel play and have difficulty sharing. They are also beginning to show assertiveness, independence and interest in the world around them. By 2 to 3 years of age, children are aware of their emotions, show their feelings in various ways, play well alongside others, need adult approval, enjoy symbolic play and imitating others, and like to please.

Language develops rapidly in the early years and all children, including those who come from language backgrounds other than English, benefit from good-quality programmes which emphasize interaction (non-verbal and verbal) and the development of communication skills. It is clear that the best programmes build on children's individual needs, interests and identities. All children acquire a first language regardless of what that language is. Babies are ready to listen and pay attention to the voices of their parents and caregivers from the first days after birth. This is strengthened through social interaction within the family (Siraj-Blatchford and Clarke 2000).

Defining language is a complex task. Gonzales-Mena (1998) defines language as 'the formation and communication of information, thoughts and feelings through the use of words'. Language learning is dependent on cognition. The main features of language are listening, speaking, reading and writing. However, non-verbal language also needs to be included and is a particularly important feature of interactions between babies and adult carers.

Acquiring a first language is a complex task. A language system is a puzzle with a variety of interlocking pieces: 'phonology' (the sounds of the language); 'vocabulary' (the words of the language); 'grammar' (the way the words are ordered and put together; 'discourse' (the way the sentences are put together; and 'pragmatics' (the rules of how to use the language) (Tabors 1997). Young children are considered to be competent in using a language when they have mastered all these pieces. This is a major task for children in the early years.

The UK Government has recently recognized the need for good-quality early communication and language development as the cornerstone of young children's learning, both social and cognitive. It is therefore not surprising that they commissioned the *Birth to Three Matters* Framework (DfES 2002). The *Birth to Three Matters* Framework has four Aspects and being A Skilful Communicator is one of them. The four Components of this Aspect are Being Together, Finding a Voice, Listening and Responding, and Making Meaning. These are subtle terms for the development of language through touch, non-verbal communication, social relations, play, and talking and listening which are responsive and meaningful for the child.

The *Birth to Three Matters* Framework (DfES 2002) also recognizes the vital role of parents/families as educators and the centrality of relationships with others, especially key, significant people like parents and childcare staff, in children's social and linguistic development. For the baby or toddler the interaction with adults and other children is vital, but these interactions do not always have to be direct and verbal. Young children use a range of their faculties, visual, olfactory and physical touch, as well as responding to a range of communication modes, language, music, movement, sound and rhythm. Therefore, all these modes are important in planning a stimulating language environment for the young child.

Early communication with babies and toddlers

The process of language development begins with the development of sounds and babbling. Initially babies are able to make a variety of sounds. By the end of the first year of life, babies can associate talk with the facial expressions of speakers, they can produce a variety of sounds that match those in their home environment or the environment they spend most time in, they can recognize the intonations of familiar people, they can take turns in conversation with adults, they can use gestures to indicate their needs, and they can respond in socially appropriate ways (Makin et al. 1995). We should not forget the important and crucial link between language and thought. Bruce (2004) reminds us of this and the need for children to communicate with other children and to communicate with adults who 'pay attention to the atmosphere they create of warmth, affection, and who send messages "you matter" ... They need adults who listen to their attempts to put their ideas, feelings and relationships into words or signs, who talk or sign with them'. Creating a warm and responsive environment for babies and toddlers is vital.

Babies are responsive to the facial expressions and sounds of the people they play with. They begin to imitate the behaviour of others and enjoy playing reciprocal vocal games, using sounds. From about the age of two months babies have been practising with a variety of sounds through their babbling. They use a combination of vowel and consonant sounds such as 'da' and 'la', which expand to sound combinations such as 'mama', 'gaga' and 'dada'. By the time they are a year old babies are using a wide variety of sounds in many combinations (Slentz and Krogh 2001). Children from different linguistic heritages all make similar babbling noises to begin with.

During the first 12 months, the most important thing for babies is touch, and voices and faces, to listen to and focus on. Adults need to remember to speak directly with the babies so they can watch the movement of their lips.

The following are important strategies for parents and practitioners to adopt to help babies and toddlers develop language:

- Make sure the babies and toddlers can see your face when you talk to them.
- Listen and respond to their language play.
- Copy the facial expressions, sounds and words made by babies and toddlers.
- Play turn-taking games.
- Sing and coo to babies, encourage sound play and babbling.
- Share pictures and objects when you talk so that a baby can identify objects with words.

- Use labelling techniques and games, for example show me your fingers, nose.
- Use plenty of repetition and imitation.
- Provide good language models.
- Keep the conversations simple.
- Encourage toddlers to say words.
- Give babies and toddlers board books and magazines to look at.
- Read stories every day.
- Make sure you have plenty of physical contact.
- Use short sentences and speak clearly.
- Involve bilingual adults and parents as much as possible.
- Encourage bilingual parents to speak their home language as much as possible.
- Learn words, rhymes and songs in other languages.
- Have lots of fun.

The *Birth to Three Matters* Framework (DfES 2002) emphasizes the need for 'being together' with others for children to become effective communicators, arguing that babies are essentially sociable. They recommend physical closeness and eye contact combined with voice to encourage 'early conversations' and the authors also recommend practitioners should be responsive in their play with babies and listen to them carefully. This 'togetherness' can be enhanced by music, mobiles above changing areas and singing of rhymes, songs and lullabies. Babies usually reciprocate when an adult is responsive to them and takes an interest in communicating with them.

Between 12 and 18 months, many babies produce first words or units of language. The first vocabulary of young children usually contains the names of people and objects, functional words such as 'no', 'mine', 'up' and 'gone', and social routines such as bye-bye. After acquiring single words, children begin to show an understanding of the early grammatical requirements of language by putting these single words together to make small sentences which express more complex relationships. This is sometimes called 'telegraphic speech'. Sometimes the same words or groups of words will have different meanings, as the following example shows:

> Anna (15 months old): milk (holds up bottle)
> Caregiver: You've finished your milk? Do you want some more?
> Anna: up.
> Caregiver: No more? You want to get out of the chair?
> > (Siraj-Blatchford and Clarke 2000)

Just like parents, caregivers can interpret the requests of young children even if their spoken language is restricted. At the same time as they are beginning to put words together, babies and toddlers are beginning to take part in interactive routines with parents and caregivers. These routines provide practice with turn-taking.

The major types of complex sentences emerge between the ages of about 2 and 4 years. Children in the early years are beginning to learn the rules of the language. On the basis of these rules they can produce and understand an infinite set of sentences. However, they will still make mistakes when they speak. They will say 'foots' instead of 'feet' and 'goed' instead of 'went'. These words are over-generalizations of rules that children are extracting from the language that they hear.

In an ideal childcare setting, babies and toddlers would hear their own language (even when this is not English) for most of the time. However, this is not always possible. As this is a crucial time for developing language, adults/parents/carers need to provide support for young learners through direct, personal communication.

It is essential to remember that communication is a two-way process, and speech is made up of a series of turns. When adults talk with children, they should provide opportunities for children to talk to them. Pauses must be left in conversations. Questions need to be simple. Children need language for developing thinking, and the more thinking they are doing the more their language will develop. At this stage, there is no need to correct pronunciation or grammar. Adults should model and expand the language used by the children (Siraj-Blatchford 1994; Clarke 1996).

The following strategies are useful for developing language in 2- to 3-year-olds:

- Read and tell stories every day.
- Develop conversations about activities.
- Plan group times to involve three or four children.
- Expand and model in conversations.
- Teach simple songs and rhymes.
- Learn rhymes and songs in other languages.
- Encourage the continued use of the home language.
- Teach lots of repetitive rhymes and games.
- Support conversations with visual materials.
- Make sure children have fun using language.

Early childhood educators and parents often regard language as the central vehicle through which children learn and make sense of their cultural environment. Language is also deeply rooted in culture and therefore a vital component of how we feel about ourselves. Children need a good image of themselves and valuing and extending their linguistic competencies and awareness is vital to this process. Self-esteem and identity are based largely on competent acquisition of language and having the language(s) we do possess recognized as valuable and acceptable. Childcare staff can help children to feel good about themselves through valuing their language(s), understanding how language develops and extending it.

By the time they are 2, most children are beginning to demonstrate the use of representational thought; this is a great leap in cognitive development. Even as young as a year old, children demonstrate through their pretend play that they can symbolize, for instance when they pretend to drink from an empty cup. The pretend play of 2-year-olds often includes familiar behaviours such as pretending to drink, eat or sleep and they often include adults, toys and pets in their play. Slentz and Krogh (2001) cite a 2-year-old who was observed offering an empty glass to her pet dog and then laughing hysterically at her own joke! Toddlers, then, are capable of combining what they have seen, heard and experienced about behaviours of people and functions of objects with social interactions, and they imitate these in everyday play.

This is not to deny that toddlers still need to develop their language and communication skills with other children and more experienced others. Many young children can be observed speaking on the telephone explaining a new toy or baby sister to the person on the other end of the phone as if the person on the phone was right there in the room with them. They often point, gesture and assume the person on the phone knows what they are pointing at or gesturing about. They also assume the person on the phone can visit them in an instant even when they might be speaking to the child from another country.

Interacting with *all* children

Siraj-Blatchford and Clarke (2000) have argued that staff need to respect all the children in their care. This means taking particular care to understand and acknowledge the different cultural and socio-economic backgrounds of the children and make special efforts to work with families to assist the children to settle into a new environment.

Boys and girls can have different language experiences within the same household. Dunn (1987) studied the relationship between mothers' conversation styles with their children aged 18–24 months. She states:

> The analysis also showed marked and consistent differences in the frequency of such conversations in families with girls and with boys. Mothers talked more to 18-month-old daughters about feeling states than they did to their 18-month-old sons. By 24 months the daughters themselves talked more about feeling states than did the sons.
>
> (1987: 37)

In multicultural or diverse societies there is a great variety of family values and traditions and interaction patterns considered to be appropriate, both verbal and non-verbal. It is important that children are brought up to balance the tensions and handle the adjustments of being reared in one way and being educated in another. Children need to become socialized into the new practices and society. Early childhood staff need to be patient, caring, tolerant, flexible and need to be able to communicate effectively with parents and other staff about their work.

In order to foster partnership and social interaction, adults who provide a good example of collaborative and cooperative practices and who facilitate a programme that acknowledges culture, language, gender and ability will be most successful. Such programmes will build on children's abilities and interests and staff will set realistic goals for children that assist them to interact with each other. Language is one of the major tools by which adults demonstrate this to children. Language increasingly becomes one of the main tools for children's social interaction.

For children entering environments in which they do not speak the language, the development of these skills and the opportunities to practise them will be more restricted unless opportunities are provided for children to use their home languages while learning English as an additional language. In the first few months, staff will need to use strategies to assist these children to enter into interactions and encourage other children to be sensitive to the needs of children learning English. The following example is adapted from Siraj-Blatchford and Clarke (2000).

When 2-and-a-half-year-old Amy entered the nursery, staff were concerned that she seemed so upset by the strange environment; by the fact no one could speak her language (Cantonese) and also that her mother seemed upset that Amy was clinging to her. The staff had already learned that Amy had only just arrived from Hong Kong after living with her grandparents while the parents tried to get established. Through an interpreter, Amy's mother explained that she would only be able to stay for the morning as she was working and her employer had said she could not take much free time. The nursery did not have a Cantonese speaker but a local resource agency was able to provide short-term bilingual support for the first few weeks. The staff in consultation with mother and the interpreter put together a strategy for supporting Amy's settlement into the nursery.

The strategy developed for Amy included:

- a session with the educator, the parents and the interpreter to fill in the bilingual enrolment form;
- a session with the staff in the toddler room, the mother and the

interpreter, to discuss Amy's usual routines at home, where she slept, her favourite toy, the languages used, any allergies or food preferences;

- an arrangement with the mother or father to bring Amy a little later each day when the other children were settled and for a parent to remain with her for a short time;
- for the parent to provide familiar food for her lunch each day;
- for the parent to bring Amy's toy that she sleeps with;
- for one staff in the nursery to be the 'significant' caregiver when Amy arrived each day;
- for a bilingual support worker to attend the nursery for the first three days and then attend on single days over the next four weeks.

Over the next few days, Amy gradually learned the routines of the centre and the staff used intervention strategies to assist Amy to mix with other children.

Practical implications for staff

Post and Hohmann (2000) argue that babies and toddlers need to feel relaxed and comfortable. They do this by being surrounded by people they know and by interesting and familiar materials and environments. We have all witnessed the impact of the key worker system or a child playing with a treasure basket, things which have become familiar to them. The consistency of the adult–child relationship and responsiveness and warmth is the foundation for successful communication. This key adult becomes the primary carer within the early years setting who provides the trusted support and love the child needs. It is within this context that the most successful interactions take place. The child comes to trust her environment and those in it.

One of the most important challenges for early childhood educators is to help children develop the skills to interact with others. Developing the social skills that assist children to get along with their peers and adults will have a significant impact on their lives. Sebastian-Nickell and Milne (1992) suggest that the development of social competence is a life-long process which begins in the first few weeks of the child's life. This process can be supported by parents and by early childhood staff. Young children need support to develop interactive skills in one to one and group situations. Even at this level, language is a major tool.

Social skills involve the strategies we use when interacting with others. They cover awareness of feelings of others. Social skills are used to enter and maintain interactions, to engage others in conversation, to maintain friendships and to cope with conflict. Non-verbal skills involve smiling, nodding, eye contact and the development of listening skills. All of these non-verbal strategies form foundations for language interactions. They vary from context to context and from culture to culture. Increased practitioner awareness of this enables stronger support to be provided for children from all backgrounds.

Time for interaction

Relationships and interactions with children should be conducted in an unhurried manner. Babies and toddlers enjoy physical contact and the interaction that goes with it, such as singing, cuddling, whispering in their ear or rocking while singing a lullaby. If a child initiates a game of peek-a-boo, the adult can join the game. Other children may prefer to observe or join in later. Children also need the time to practise their love of repetition through hearing the same songs and rhymes, banging saucepan lids, filling and emptying a container.

Music and movement

Build a repertoire of songs, lullabies (these can calm babies and toddlers) and rhymes to sing with the children. The repetitive nature of these will enhance language development. Adults can sing unaccompanied or spontaneously as well as with the children, which helps children to identify the adult's voice and to take an interest in the sounds or join in. Taped music can be used occasionally to add variety. Staff in bilingual settings should try and ensure songs and rhymes are sung from the child's home language as well. Clapping and moving to music and words is a fun way of developing language and listening. Do not encourage background music in an early childhood setting as this adds to noise levels and has little purpose. As children get older they will enjoy the more physical aspects of mixing music, movement and songs/ rhymes, such as moving to slow and faster beats on a drum to the rhyme 'bananas with pyjamas'. Similarly, patting knees, clapping hands or using chime bars can set a beat which copies the rhythm of words and also helps children to maintain attention. Try using small groups during the music and singing experiences and encourage children to sing alone, as well as doing this yourself!

Let the child lead

In the past a great deal of emphasis was put on observing children or watching them. Most early childhood educators are now agreed that it is equally important to listen to children. This is especially true of babies and toddlers, but the listener and watcher has to be very patient and understanding. Young children rely heavily on adults being patient listeners. By watching and listening to children we learn to get to their physical level, to respect the materials they enjoy and join in, to follow their pace and interests and in particular to respond appropriately to their expressions, noises and words. Very young children rely heavily on non-verbal cues and the adult has to be alert, responsive and patient.

Listening and responding

Listening and responding relies heavily on reciprocal behaviour. Babies respond well to making everyday activities fun. The *Birth to Three Matters* Framework (DfES 2002) gives a number of examples such as using puppets and props alongside stories and songs, as well as physical fun through dressing time, like waiting for fingers to pop out of sleeves or a head through a vest. Children with communication learning difficulties or those from language communities other than English will require even greater support and reliance on non-verbal smiles, patience, thoughtful and positive, warm responses from the adults who care for them. Keeping conversations simple is important and helping babies and toddlers by naming objects they are familiar with helps them to make connections even before they can speak the words. The models of language that the adults supply should be good models. For example, if a child holds up his bottle and says 'milk' the adult can respond by saying 'You want more milk?' 'I will give you more milk'. If toddlers make mistakes, the adult should just say the same thing back to them, but model the target utterance. For example, if a toddler says 'adpol' (while pointing at a tadpole), the adult should say 'Yes, that's right, it's a tadpole'.

Sustained shared thinking

From the research on interactions with babies and toddlers, cited in this chapter, it is evident that babies and young children need sustained, shared interactions with adults and other children (both verbal and non-verbal). A sustained interaction may not necessarily be for as long a time as is possible with over 3s but an appropriate interaction such as a peek-a-boo game may last for some time when both parties are enjoying it! Any kind of sustained interaction will lead to greater skills in communication and ultimately to enhanced thinking skills too. The same study found that very few open-ended questions were asked of pre-schoolers. Making a running commentary, or acknowledging what children are doing, trying to say or feeling, is fine, but sometimes open-ended questions (when we are looking at, say, a choice of activities from the child's point of view) are also important. If the child is preverbal the adult can gently and calmly state the options she has and watch for non-verbal responses, such as pointing to a particular toy or activity. This will help children to make choices and encourage empathy on the part of the adult. An important part of the *Birth to Three Matters* Framework (DfES 2002) is Meaning Making. Understanding and being understood takes time. Even adults know this, especially when we are finding it hard to find the right words! Trust and support is necessary, and creating a climate that offers supportive, child-focused interactions to young children is vital.

References

Bruce, T. (2004) *Developing Learning in Early Childhood*. London: Paul Chapman Publishing.

Clarke, P. (1992) *English as a Second Language in Early Childhood*. Victoria: Free Kindergarten Association.

Clarke, P. (1996) Investigating second language acquisition in preschools: a longitudinal study of four Vietnamese-speaking four year olds acquisition of English, unpublished Ph.D. thesis, LaTrobe University.

DfES (2002) *Birth to Three Matters*. London: DfES Publications.

Dunn, J. (1987) Understanding feelings: the early stages, in J. Bruner and H. Haste (eds) *Making Sense: The Child's Construction of the World*. New York: Methuen.

Gonzales-Mena, J. (1998) *Foundations: Early Childhood Education in a Diverse Society*. California: Mayfield Publishing Company.

Makin, L., Campbell, J. and Jones Diaz, C. (1995) *One Childhood, Many Languages*. Sydney: Harper Educational.

Post, J. and Hohmann, M. (2000) *Tender Care and Early Learning: Supporting Infants and Toddlers in Child Care Settings*. Michigan: High/Scope Press.

Sebastian–Nickell, P. and Milne, R. (1992) *Care and Education of Young Children*. Melbourne: Longman.

Siraj-Blatchford, I. (1994) *The Early Years: Laying the Foundations for Racial Equality*. Stoke on Trent: Trentham Books.

Siraj-Blatchford, I. and Clarke, P. (2000) *Supporting Identity, Diversity and Language in the Early Years*. Buckingham: Open University Press.

Slentz, K.L. and Krogh, S.L. (2001) *Early Childhood Development and its Variations*. New Jersey: Lawrence Erlbaum Associates.

Tabors, P.O. (1997) *One Child, Two Languages*. Baltimore: Paul Brookes Publishing.

Trevarthen, C. (1992) An infant's motives for thinking and speaking in the culture, in A.H. Wold (ed.) *The Dialogical Alternative*. Oxford: Oxford University Press, pp. 99–137.

13 Creativity Matters

Bernadette Duffy

Introduction

Bernadette Duffy has been closely associated with the development of the *Birth to Three Matters* Framework (DfES 2002). As a member of the Working Group which met regularly at Coram Family, and as Head of the Thomas Coram Early Childhood Centre located on the same site, she played a key role in hosting meetings, organizing photo shoots and allowing videoing to take place. Her commitment to fostering and supporting creativity and imagination is evident both in her practice and in her writing. In this chapter she discusses the work of the Thomas Coram Centre for Children and Families.

In this chapter I will be sharing the work of the Thomas Coram Centre for Children and Families. The Thomas Coram Centre is a partnership between Coram Family, one of the oldest children's charities in this country, and the London Borough of Camden. The centre works with children from birth [and before] and their parents in a number of ways and offers a range of services for the birth to 3 age group. These services include full- and part-week group provision in the nursery, drop-ins which children attend with their parents and carers, crèches, a childminder network, toy library, music sessions and community outreach offering home visits. Practitioners, children and parents at Thomas Coram were involved in the development of the *Birth to Three Matters* Framework (DfES 2002) in a number of ways, including acting as members of the Steering and Working Groups, participating in practitioner and parent consultation groups and as the subjects of video materials. We are also very fortunate to be part of the Esmée Fairbairn-funded *Birth to Three Training Matters* project (described more fully in Chapter 14) and so have our own Advanced Skills Practitioner to help us implement the Framework.

The site occupied by the centre has a history of supporting young children stretching back to the eighteenth century and part of its tradition has been an emphasis on the visual and performing arts. We are eager to maintain and develop this focus, and as we have been implementing the *Birth to Three Matters* Framework we have been particularly interested in the role of creativity and the arts in the lives of the youngest children. In this chapter I will look at how we are addressing this and exploring the following issues:

- why we think creativity is important;
- creativity across the *Birth to Three Matters* Framework (DfES 2002);
- examples of the links between creativity and the different Aspects and Components of the *Birth to Three Matters* Framework (DfES 2002);
- the creative process;
- creativity and children from birth to 3;
- the role of the adult in promoting creativity; for example, creating conditions that inspire creativity and developing creativity through our interactions with children;
- creativity in action, examples of practice at Thomas Coram.

My aim in this chapter is to explore the rich opportunities we have to support the creativity of our youngest children or, as a colleague put it, 'there is more to creativity than cutting the legs off the easel so that the youngest children can reach'.

Why we think creativity is important

Being creative is important to all of us. It supports us in exploring the full range of human potential and improves our capacity for thought and action. It enables us to respond to a rapidly changing world by reappraising our values and ways of working. The creative process helps us to deal with the unexpected by extending our current knowledge to new situations and using information in new ways. It encourages us to take risks, think flexibly, be innovative, play with ideas and respond imaginatively.

We are all creative. Recent thinking distinguishes between 'big c' and 'little c' creativity. 'Big c' creativity involves invention and a break with past understanding, for example the creative process that Einstein engaged in. 'Little c' creativity enables individuals to find routes and paths to travel (Craft 2001). It is a process of conscious invention and describes the resourcefulness of ordinary people rather than extraordinary contributors. It is the sort of creativity we all need every day of our lives and this includes the youngest children.

Creativity across the *Birth to Three Matters* Framework

Birth to Three Matters (DfES 2002) stresses the importance of promoting children's creativity from their earliest years. Frequently creativity is seen as simply the visual and performing arts, such as drawing, painting, music and dance. The assumption is that if children are involved in the arts they are automatically being creative. However, this is not always the case. Involvement in the arts does not necessarily mean involvement in creativity. Many art experiences offered to young children are dull, repetitive and far from creative; a way of occupying children and making things to cover the walls rather than a way of promoting creativity. The arts do have an important role in promoting creativity and we have all seen how much babies and young children enjoy music, dance and opportunities to explore paint and other materials, but these are not the only ways to promote creativity. Every Aspect and Component of the *Birth to Three Matters* Framework (DfES 2002) has the potential to offer creative experiences Table 13.1. Being creative is just as much part of being A Strong Child as being A Competent Learner.

Young children are being creative when they:

- use materials in new ways;
- combine previously unconnected materials;
- make discoveries that are new to them;
- create something new and original for them.

The creative process

The Framework encourages us to support children as they engage in the creative process. This process includes:

- Curiosity or 'What is it'? This is when children are alert, interested, want to know more, and it is clear that their attention has been captured.
- Exploration or 'What can and does it do?' Children can be observed actively investigating objects, events or ideas, using all their senses to gather information, and watching others can also be part of their investigation.
- Play or 'What can I do with this?' Children initiate a period of total immersion characterized by spontaneity and often without clear final objectives. As there is little or no focus on a predetermined product, they are free to examine all kinds of detail during this period that they may have missed if they had been concentrating on

Table 13.1 Examples of the links between creativity and the different Aspects and Components

A Strong Child	A Skilful Communicator
■ Me, Myself and I	■ Being Together
■ Being Acknowledged and Affirmed	■ Finding a Voice
■ Developing Self-assurance	■ Listening and Responding
■ A Sense of Belonging	■ Making Meaning
Taking part in activities such as exploring paint in a group gives children shared experiences, which helps their sense of belonging.	The visual and performing arts offer opportunities for communication that does not rely on words. This helps children to share their feelings and ideas and to understand other children's.
Developing the ability to imagine enables children to put themselves in someone else's position, which helps to create the conditions for friendships.	Imaginative play offers meaningful opportunities to listen and pay attention to others.

A Competent Learner	A Healthy Child
■ Making Connections	■ Emotional Well-being
■ Being Imaginative	■ Growing and Developing
■ Being Creative	■ Keeping Safe
■ Representing	■ Healthy Choices
The creative process is all about making connections, representing ideas and being imaginative.	Children express their feelings through their representations, such as imaginative play.
Through involvement in imaginative play, children develop and extend their ability to imagine. Children can develop their own ways of representing their ideas and sharing them with others.	The creative process encourages the ability to solve problems and to persist with challenges. This helps to develop a sense of mastery or resilience in the child, which is closely linked to well-being. Involvement in the visual and performing arts gives plenty of opportunities to develop physical skills in a meaningful way.

the end product. This is an opportunity to practise and consolidate the skills and knowledge they have acquired in the earlier levels.

- Creativity or 'What can I create or invent?' The child discovers uncommon or new approaches to the materials or problem they are investigating; they take risks and make new connections.

Creativity and children from birth to 3

Observations of babies and young children show that they are eager to engage in the creative process. They are naturally curious about the world around them and want to explore it.

Babies' brains are designed to enable them to make sense of the world around them. As they use their senses to explore the world they find themselves in, they create mental images and this helps them to make sense of new experiences by comparing them to the images they already have. As more of these images are created, connections form between them and these enable the child to form new understandings. Creativity means connecting the previously unconnected in ways that are new and meaningful to the individual concerned (Duffy 1998). Recent research has established that more connections are made in the first years of life than at any other time. The creative process helps children to make these connections by enabling them to:

- explore, comprehend and develop their understanding of the world around them;
- communicate their feelings in non-verbal and pre-verbal ways and to express their thoughts;
- think about and create new meanings;
- to solve problems, gain mastery and gain self-esteem;
- experience beauty;
- create a view of the world that is uniquely their own.

Watching the youngest children shows us that they have persistent concerns with aspects of the world around them that they are keen to explore. While many children's interests reflect schemas such as 'enveloping' and 'transporting' (Bruce 1997), others seem to reflect the children's experiences of a widening world. Some of the ones we have noticed are listed below:

- light, movement and sound;
- materials and their properties, especially food, sand, water;
- everyday objects, such as cups, spoons, tins, brushes;
- home roles and activities, such as cooking, washing, cleaning;

- babies, especially bathing, feeding and dressing;
- animals, such as pets, farm and zoo animals;
- transport and community roles, such as police, post person, shops;
- people, faces, spaces.

We use this understanding of children's persistent concerns to plan the environment we offer and the experiences we provide. Through their increasing physical and linguistic abilities young children are able to explore an ever-widening world. They do not leave behind the interests of earlier stages but add to these to develop an increasingly complex view of the world and their relationship to it. As children progress, their ability to engage in creative and imaginative experience increases. In turn, the projection into an imaginary world stretches their conceptual abilities and involves a development in their abstract thought (Vygotsky 1978).

The role of the adult in promoting creativity

In order to take on new challenges, children need to be secure and to experience intimate relationships with adults who can understand the world from their view-point and mediate between the child and the outside world. Adults have a key role in supporting and extending children's creativity; we have the power to help or hinder.

Create conditions that inspire creativity inside and outside:

- Connecting the previously unconnected is a key aspect of creativity, and the environment we create needs to give the children the opportunity to do this, for example by enabling them to move and transport resources and materials and combine them in new ways.
- Practitioners should pay particular attention to creating an environment which stimulates children's creativity, originality and expressiveness. Curiosity is a key part of the creative process. If children are not in an environment that excites their curiosity and encourages them to explore and play, they will not be creative.
- The range of resources and organization we provide will determine what, and how, the children can create and how creative they can be. Creativity is about making meaningful connections, using ideas and/ or materials in new ways. Our organization of space and resources will largely determine whether children can do this. Each setting will offer its own possibilities. As practitioners we need to look at our setting and maximize its potential for creativity.
- For the youngest children we need to give particular attention to

accessibility and ensure that present opportunities for creativity match the development of the child.

This could be done by:

- Providing resources either on the floor or in treasure baskets containing an abundance of interesting natural and household objects, for pre-mobile children (Goldschmied and Jackson 1994). Mobiles and mirrors are also a means of bringing the world to the youngest children.
- Ensuring that furniture is solid and stable to support the explorations of just mobile children.
- Providing opportunities to explore that reflect growing mobility such as heuristic play. This involves providing plenty of materials such as tubes, tins, chains, corks, for filling and emptying, fitting things into containers, banging, shaking, pushing and pulling (Goldschmied and Jackson 1994).
- Developing what children have learned during heuristic play sessions by encouraging their interest in transporting objects and materials and enabling them to connect the previously unconnected.
- Extending the resources into the outside space to match the exploratory desire of increasingly mobile children and giving them the opportunity to move freely between the inside and outside.
- Reflecting children's increasing interest in the roles they see the adults around them engage in by offering plenty of opportunities for exploring these through imaginative play.

Developing creativity through our interactions with children

Children's attitudes are greatly influenced by the adults around them. If we want to encourage children's creativity, we need to use our own. Practitioners need to:

- use their imagination to make learning more interesting, exciting, and effective;
- take risks;
- leave the security of structured activities behind;
- learn from the children.

The findings of the Effective Provision of Pre School Education Project (EPPE 2003) has helped us at Thomas Coram to develop our thinking about teaching for creativity by focusing on the importance of adult–child inter-actions. For the youngest children many of these interactions will not consist of words alone and will involve the adult tuning into the child's gestures, sounds and body language. At this stage in their development children need adults who appreciate the idiosyncratic nature of their communications and can help them communicate outside their 'magic circle' of parents, siblings and close friends. Our aim is to encourage periods of *sustained-shared thinking* which develop and extend the child's understanding. Sustained-shared thinking happens when practitioners and children 'work together' in an intellectual way, for example to solve a problem, clarify a concept, evaluate an activity, extend a narrative. Adult 'modelling', when the practitioner models through demonstration, is often combined with sustained periods of shared thinking, as are open-ended questions and comments. Children's freely chosen play offers many opportunities to promote learning when practitioners recognize its importance and interact with children while they play.

Naomi, who is 1 year old, approaches her key worker, Phil, with two circular pieces of wood. Phil accepts them and sits on the floor beside Naomi who is looking attentively at the wooden circles. 'I wonder what happens if I tap them?' says Phil, gently tapping the wood. Naomi reaches out and takes them, taps them and hands them back to Phil. 'I wonder what happens if I rub them?' and Phil rubs them together. Again Naomi reaches and takes the wooden circles then rubs them. She hands them back to Phil, who starts to spin them on the floor. Naomi watches as they spin, wobble, and then fall to the floor with a clatter. Laughing, she grabs them and hands them to Phil who repeats the spinning, saying 'they're spinning, spinning ... oh no, starting to wobble ... down they go!' After Phil has repeated this a few times Naomi takes the wooden circles and tries to spin them herself. She concentrates hard and repeats the exercise until finally they spin and fall to the floor with a satisfying clatter. Naomi looks up at Phil, points to the circles, and claps her hands with pleasure.

Our day-to-day interactions with children offer many opportunities to promote creativity. We can encourage children's creativity by:

- valuing each child's representations as unique and personal to her/him;
- helping each child to feel secure – creativity grows when children feel secure enough to take risks and make mistakes;
- being available, interested and involved with the children;
- learning together – let the children see you trying new things;
- recognizing that the process may be more important than the product on some occasions;

- showing the children how to use new materials and equipment;
- emphasizing exploration and active participation;
- knowing when to be silent, when to encourage, when to inspire and when to help;
- pausing before speaking and giving the child the opportunity to speak first;
- being genuine and honest; praising everything a child does is not being honest, but offering constructive feedback and encouragement is;
- seeing the world through the eyes of children.

Creativity in action – examples of practice at Thomas Coram

During the last few years at Thomas Coram we have been using our observations of the children and our developing understanding of research to help us plan, implement and assess experiences that promote creativity in the youngest children. Here are some of the ways we have tried to do this.

Example 1

At Thomas Coram we support the view that children learn about the world around them through their senses and the physical manipulation of their environment. Practitioners working with babies observed their fascination with water, whether watching the rain trickle down the window or putting their hands under the running taps to see what happened. They decide to build on this interest by focusing on water exploration and encouraging the children to explore water in its many forms and situations, including the following experiences.

- Practitioners froze large pieces of ice and placed these on trays on the floor for the children to observe and investigate.
- Hand washing provided ideal opportunities for creative exploration, including turning taps on and off, finding out how the water makes the soap foam, discovering that warm water comes from one tap and cold from the other. The children had plenty of opportunities to predict, experiment and formulate new theories.
- The garden gave children the chance to explore water in the environment, for example splashing in puddles, watching the rain drip from the trees and watering plants.
- Large trays filled with water encouraged children to immerse themselves in water and explore using all their senses. This led to high levels of involvement.
- The children 'painted' using buckets filled with water and brushes. They watched as the surface changed as the sun dried the water.

Practitioners supported the children's creativity by providing appropriate resources, interacting with the children as they explored and introducing new words and resources as needed. At the end of the exploration they produced a booklet documenting the children's exploration in words and pictures to share with parents and colleagues.

Example 2

During her observations of a group of 2- and 3-year-olds Sam noticed that they were far more interested in exploring the properties of the glue she had provided for them rather than using it to stick the materials available in the workshop. Sam decided to encourage this exploration. She set aside a table covered in a plastic sheet for the glue exploration. The glue was available to the children throughout the day and was left overnight ready for them to continue their exploration the next day. Over the next few days the children poured and dripped glue on the plastic sheet. They added other materials to the glue – food colouring, glitter and bits of paper – to see what happened. As the glue dried, the children observed that it changed from opaque to clear and they could see the different materials embedded in the layers. This process went on for over a week.

The practitioners observed the children as they created the glue surface and recorded the children's development in the different Aspects and Components of the *Birth to Three Matters* Framework (DfES 2002). For example, the children worked together as a group promoting their development as skilful communicators. They developed dispositions such as persistence and concentration, thus promoting emotional well-being. They explored the properties of materials and developed their knowledge and understanding of the world around them, encouraging their development as competent learners. The children were given time and space to explore. Their ideas were valued and responded to, which reinforced their sense of themselves as strong children.

Example 3

After listening to a story about a child helping his parent to make things with wood, a group of 2- and 3-year-olds at the centre wanted to try this for themselves. Marcia, their key person, realized that this was a good time to introduce the children to a new set of skills. This group had not used wood and woodwork tools before and the practitioners thought about how best to help them develop their ability to use new materials and tools. They considered the particular needs of the individual children in the group, which included children with special educational needs and children for whom English was an additional language. Parents and practitioners spent time with each child introducing them to wood, saws, hammers and nails. They modelled for the children ways to use the tools safely and then scaffolded the children as they acquired the skills for themselves. As the children's confidence grew they decided to work together, joining their individual bits of wood to create a structure. The adults involved were aware of the importance of keeping a balance between adult- and child-initiated activities. They showed the children how to use the new materials and tools and, once the children had mastered these, they supported them in using their new skills to produce a structure based on their own ideas.

Conclusion

As adults we have a key role to play in the development of the creativity of the very youngest children. To do this we need to try to see the world through the eyes of the child and rediscover the magic and excitement that comes from experiencing things for the first time. If we can do this we will enrich the lives of the children and our own.

Acknowledgements

Many thanks to Linda Happe, Marcia Fraser and Janice Marshall for their help in writing this chapter.

References

Bruce, T. (1997) *Early Childhood Education*. London: Hodder and Stoughton.

Craft, A. (2001) Little c creativity, in A. Craft, B. Jeffrey and M. Leibling (eds) *Creativity in Education*. London: Continuum.

DfES (2002) *Birth to Three Matters*. London: DfES Publications.

Duffy, B. (1998) *Supporting Creativity and Imagination in the Early Years*. Milton Keynes: Open University Press.

Effective Provision of Pre School Education (EPPE) (2003) *Findings from the Pre-school Period Summary of Findings*. London: Institute of Education, University of London.

Goldschmied, E. and Jackson, S. (1994) *People Under Three: Young Children and Day Care*. London: Routledge and Kegan Paul.

Vygotsky, L. (1978) *Mind in Society*. Cambridge, Mass.: Harvard University Press.

14 Training Matters

Lesley Abbott and Ann Langston

Introduction

Training matters have played a key role in the professional lives of both Lesley Abbott and Ann Langston. Responsibility for training students at very different rungs on the 'climbing frame', involvement in course development and leadership, research into teaching requirements, writing and lobbying for appropriate funded training has equipped them with knowledge and awareness of the issues. In this chapter they share their concerns whilst highlighting new training developments and initiatives.

Training matters

Training to work in any field matters greatly, but especially in the early years, an ever-expanding field with an increasing number of associated posts in a wide range of childcare contexts. In the UK, initial training for work with young children ranges from introductory courses for individuals wishing to find out whether childcare is for them, to courses up to Level 4 and beyond. Additionally there are courses at first-degree level, which often build on prior experience and learning such as the Early Years Sector Endorsed Foundation degrees, Early Childhood Studies degrees and B.A., B.Ed. and Masters degrees. Whilst some qualifications can stand alone, in reality many form progression routes which individuals, who wish to do so, may follow over a period of time, alongside their practical work in an early childhood setting. Inevitably the speed of change in the early years, the introduction of the *Birth to Three Matters* Framework (DfES 2002) and an increasing recognition that work with the very youngest children from birth to 3 years is profoundly significant has led to a greater need to focus on both initial and continuing professional development for staff.

It has long been argued that the key to quality experiences and provision for young children depends upon the quality of the adults who work with them and the appropriateness of the training they receive (DES 1990; Ball 1994; Hevey and Curtis 1996; Abbott and Pugh 1998; Abbott and Hevey 2001). Providers and practitioners alike have identified the need for affordable, accessible, appropriate training. A 'climbing frame' model of training (Abbott and Pugh 1998) recognized the need for training, which supports practitioners at various stages in their professional lives and is sufficiently flexible to meet their requirements and those of the setting or sector in which they work. This model has subsequently been developed as a *Framework of Nationally Accredited Qualifications for Early Years Education, Childcare and Play Work* (QCA 1999) and the *Framework for Higher Education Qualifications* (QAA 2001), ensuring clear progression routes, which support training providers in planning their training, and practitioners in identifying which courses they wish to follow.

An issue emphasized by the introduction of *Birth to Three Matters* (DfES 2002) is the need for targeted training for work with children from birth to 3, an area often considered the 'Cinderella' of childcare, unattractive because of the lack of opportunities for promotion and progression, and often the area where young trainees are placed, with posts caring for older children preferentially allocated to more mature members of staff. The issue here concerns both the image that work with the very youngest children reflects, and the value and status placed on it by managers and policy makers. What seems necessary is that they, and practitioners, recognize that work with the very youngest children is, if anything, more important than work with older children, because it is in the very earliest weeks and months of their lives that babies learn about themselves and other people and, depending upon what they learn, begin to form views of whether they are loveable or unloveable. So, arguably, work with very young children is highly significant and deserves the best trained people, yet it is also often underrated.

In view of this, and the recognition on the part of many practitioners that training and support would be necessary in order to successfully implement the *Birth to Three Matters* Framework (DfES 2002), funding to develop a small-scale project was sought by the team at Manchester Metropolitan University (MMU). This resulted in the Esmée Fairbairn-funded research project, which was undertaken (by the authors of this chapter) with five high-quality centres throughout England. The focus was on exploring the roles of early years practitioners working with children between birth and 3 in out of home care. In consequence a model similar to that used in the Foundation Stage, in which Early Years and/or Advanced Skills Teachers were available in many local authorities to provide support and guidance to staff working with children aged from 3 to 5 years, was adopted. Early years practitioners, under the guidance of a Researcher/Mentor, were trained as Advanced Skills Practitioners (ASPs) to work within and beyond their own setting supporting those working with babies and young children, in out of home care, to implement the *Birth to Three Matters* Framework (DfES 2002). Since no similar role existed to support those working with children from birth to 3, this was an innovative approach and one which, it was thought, met the needs of many practitioners for accessible training for work with this age group.

Consultation revealed that the nature of support needed by practitioners in out of home care with children up to 3 years should, of necessity, be local, community-based and flexible to accommodate the diverse needs of workers, whilst sympathetic to individual patterns of work and family life. At the same time, it should support their development as professionals, provide access to training and qualifications and enhance the provision of high-quality play and learning activities for children up to the age of 3 in non-statutory settings, through more effective practice and access to wider resources.

The project set out to create a practice model to support the aims above, and to record the process in order to assess its capability for replication on a wider scale in the future. This work is still in progress, but at the end of the first phase enormous benefits have been derived and the successes of this project include the following factors, which it is believed will be influential in expanding the boundaries of perceptions about the possibilities of work with this age group:

- A recognition by the DfES/Sure Start Unit of the exemplary work being undertaken in several of the centres involved in this project.[1]
- Fact-finding visits from DfES personnel to Newcastle to visit one of the research centres: Cruddas Park Centre, Newcastle.[2]
- Preliminary development of a module, *Birth to Three Matters*, based on the new Framework of Effective Practice, which is to be offered on the CACHE Diploma in Pre-School Practice.
- *Birth to Three Matters* ongoing module development between Cruddas Park Centre and Northumbria University entitled *Aspects in Care and Education: Managing People*.[3]
- Conferences based around *Birth to Three Matters* (DfES 2002) involving project team and researchers as keynote speakers and/or in information giving.
- Sharing of information between all project members on important issues such as planning, ways of using materials, resources and people and/or organizations to contact. The Project's centres were described in a letter to Local Authority Early Years Development and Childcare Partnership (EYDCP) Lead Officers. This letter refers to centres that are 'already developing innovative training and wider dissemination programmes'.

The first phase of this project has provided evidence of ways in which the *Birth to Three Matters* (DfES 2002) materials are influencing planning and are being used successfully with parents and other community members. The second phase of the project will focus on the production of video and re-source materials to support practitioners in using the Framework.

Birth to Three Matters, **Training of Trainers**

Whilst the results of the Esmée Fairbairn project have been successful in the relatively small number of centres and localities involved, it was clear that a larger training project would be required to meet the needs of practitioners nationally. Following the launch of the *Birth to Three Matters* Framework (DfES 2002) and the introduction of the materials, delegates to nine regional con-ferences, led by MMU, on behalf of the Department for Education and Skills (DfES)/Sure Start Unit, consistently requested that a programme of training should follow so that the benefit of introducing the framework would not be lost, through lack of understanding on behalf of trainers. As a result, after a tendering exercise, the DfES/Sure Start Unit contracted MMU to prepare a programme of Training of Trainers to be accompanied by Childcare Work-force Training materials to support trainers when they began to train the childcare workforce.

To this end, comprehensive materials were developed, and a further series of conferences took place in the nine government regions for approximately seven hundred representatives from groups identified by the SSU, including EYDCPs, Further Education (FE), Learning Skills Council (LSCs) and health teams in Sure Start programmes.

The Training of Trainers programme included the following aims:

For participants (training personnel) to:

1. Develop an understanding of the materials in the *Birth to Three Matters* (DfES 2002) pack, in order to be able to deliver training to a range of their colleagues involved in training in their local authority.
2. Know and understand the aims and principles that underpin the *Birth to Three Matters* Framework (DfES 2002) and how these link to wider early childhood principles including the Foundation Stage principles.
3. Know and understand how, and why, the Framework characterizes children and defines their development in broad areas.
4. Develop an understanding of how issues relating to special needs are addressed in the Framework, and how these can be used in sup-porting practitioners in the identification and assessment of children with special needs and disabilities.
5. Develop an awareness of ways to promote effective practice with under 3s through the use of the *Birth to Three Matters* (DfES 2002).
6. Develop an understanding of ways to implement the Framework

practically in a range of individual settings such as childminders' homes, full daycare, group settings and pre-schools, taking particular account of issues of diversity.

7. Develop an understanding of the links made in the framework to the Foundation Stage and the National Standards for Under Eights Day Care and Childminding.

8. Become familiar with the Training of Trainer's materials so that they are able to use them in training other trainers in their own EYDCP.

9. Understand how this training relates to the underpinning knowledge required for the National Occupational Standards.

Aims 1 to 4 were to be achieved through a six-hour distance learning study programme and aims 5 to 9 were to be studied at a training event which took place, as described, in one of the nine government regions.

Birth to Three Matters, training the Childcare Workforce

In parallel with the training described, the Childcare Workforce materials were also developed. The aims of these mirrored closely those of the Training of Trainers programme, although they were presented so that they would be simple to use, and many were offered at several levels to reflect the different levels of knowledge held by practitioners. The Childcare Workforce materials were sent to all Partnership Lead Officers for distribution to trainers in each local authority. These materials should be a useful tool for trainers, and of benefit to practitioners, however, whilst they will undoubtedly contribute to relevant underpinning knowledge for the purposes of National Vocational Qualifications (NVQs), in themselves as yet they are insufficient to constitute a validated training course.

It is important that further developments take place in order to include *Birth to Three Matters* training in validated courses.

Further and Higher Education and Awarding Bodies Events

In view of this difficulty, and in recognition of the impact of the *Birth to Three Matters* Framework (DfES 2002) for training, a 'discussion' has begun between the SSU, the MMU *Birth to Three Matters* project team and all awarding bodies and further education and higher education institutions (FE/HEIs) in England, with an interest in early years, to address the changes, which must result from the introduction of the Framework.

This 'discussion' will take the form of three events to which some of the groups identified above will send delegates to learn more about the *Birth to*

Three Matters Framework (DfES 2002) itself; to be informed about the *Birth to Three Matters* Training (of trainers and practitioners), that has taken place since its introduction; to assess and understand the impact on employment and practice that the Framework has made, and to share information about how the Framework can become embedded into courses, awards and qualifications.

Every FE/HEI in England, offering early years courses together with any awarding bodies who do so, have been invited to attend one of the events, which will also be attended by representatives from the Sure Start Unit, employers, members of National Occupational Standards review team and the *Birth to Three Matters* project team from MMU. It is hoped that the discussions will both highlight the need and indicate the process by which the *Birth to Three Matters* Framework (DfES 2002) can, in the future, be fully reflected in courses, qualifications and awards, so that trainees will be enabled to develop an in-depth understanding of the aims, principles and practice espoused in the Framework. This will be the first step on a long journey which we hope will lead to a greater understanding of work in the early years, the proliferation of an increasing number of accredited courses relating to babies and young children and a growing interest in training to work with them.

Conclusion

This book is about *Birth to Three Matters*, of which training is probably one of the most important matters, since all other matters either stem from, or are integral to, this issue. Currently the way forward for training in terms of *Birth to Three Matters* is still being negotiated and will, in time, we hope, come to be reflected in the content and assessment of award-bearing and accredited courses. However, it is important to stress that in order to do justice to the content of such courses that both they and the associated National Occupational Standards (NOS) should be subject to extensive scrutiny, question and revision so that they begin to reflect the complexity of work with babies and young children as well as the fact that their care and development does not occur separately, but that the two are interdependent.

To some extent some of these points have begun to be addressed through this book. For example, in Chapter 10, Peter Elfer argues that observation can never be objective and that far from detracting from the process, accepting that emotions are involved, when we observe children, allows us to more fully understand what it is that we have observed. Similarly, we are reminded by Tina Bruce, Iram Siraj-Blatchford and Bernadette Duffy that play, interaction and creativity are fundamental to children's well-being and development; processes which are easily overlooked in the 'busyness' of managing children's care in out of home settings.

Training to care for and educate young children is a complex task, which must provide trainees with real understandings of many things, including the importance of inclusion discussed by Julie Jennings. Similarly, anti-discriminatory practice and children's safety, on which John Powell has focused, remind us that young children are in need of protection not only from harmful environments but also from psychological harm. It must also encourage practitioners to recognize that, as Helen Moylett and Pat Djemli remind us, practitioners also matter, and that their own physical and mental well-being is paramount in work with young children. It is also noteworthy that whilst such work is rewarding, it is also frequently demanding and challenging, sometimes leaving practitioners with more questions than answers, and faced with dilemmas to which there appear to be few solutions. Discussion with colleagues and awareness of the current early years climate is important in facing some of these challenges.

We believe that the best start for every early years practitioner, whether a trainee or an old hand at the job, is to become familiar with the vast body of research, which Tricia David and Kathy Goouch have begun to discuss in Chapter 4. At the same time we would encourage them to try to keep abreast of the increasing amount of literature that continues to reveal to us so much about babies' and young children's early competence.

This discussion will continue in many early childhood forums. The publication by the Government of the Green Paper *Every Child Matters* (HM Treasury 2003) provides further issues for debate. It shares many of the goals for children with *Birth to Three Matters* (DfES 2002). The five outcomes for children and young people outlined in the Green Paper (HM Treasury 2003) – being healthy, staying safe, enjoying and achieving, making a positive contribution and economic well-being – echo the Aspects and Components of the *Birth to Three Matters* Framework (DfES 2002).

The challenge now is to recognize that, as the Green Paper states, 'everyone in our society has a responsibility for securing these outcomes' (HM Treasury 2003: 14).

Perhaps the most fundamental understandings early years practitioners need are those that relate to quality in early years settings and how they can promote and influence its development when all around them people have such different perspectives about what 'quality' looks like. We have begun this debate in Chapter 6.

Notes

[1] Sure Start Letter dated 31 July 2003
[2] Excerpt of Report
[3] Module Outline, University of Northumbria

References

Abbott, L. and Hevey, D. (2001) Training to work in the early years, in G. Pugh (ed.) *Contemporary Issues in the Early Years*. London: Paul Chapman Publishing in association with Coram Family.

Abbott, L. and Pugh, G. (1998) *Training to Work in the Early Years: Developing the Climbing Frame*. Buckingham: Open University Press.

Ball, C. (1994) *Start Right – The Importance of Early Learning*. London: Royal Society for the Encouragement of Arts, Manufacturers and Commerce.

DES (1990) *Starting with Quality, Report of the Committee of Inquiry into the Quality of the Educational Experiences Offered to 3 and 4 Year Olds, Chaired by Mrs Angela Rumbold CBE*. London: HMSO.

DfES (2002) *Birth to Three Matters*. London: DfES Publications.

Hevey, D. and Curtis, A. (1996) Training to work in the early years, in G. Pugh (ed.) *Contemporary Issues in the Early Years*, 2nd edn. London: Paul Chapman.

HM Treasury (2003) *Every Child Matters*. London: The Stationery Office.

Langston, A. (2004) *Birth to Three Matters, Training of Trainers, Final Report*, 7 May. Manchester: Manchester Metropolitan University.

Langston, A. and Abbott, L. (2004) *Birth to Three Training Matters, Interim Report, Esmée Fairbairn/Manchester Metropolitan University Research Project*. Manchester: Manchester Metropolitan University.

QAA (2001) *The Framework of Higher Education Qualifications in England Wales and Northern Ireland*. London: QAA.

QCA (1999) *Early Years Education, Childcare and Playwork. A Framework of Nationally Accredited Qualifications*. London: QCA.

Index